Pauline

DEBT RESCUE

Duffetted!

DEBT RESCUE

*How to Get Through a Year of Financial Ruin...
and Survive!*

Gary Webster

*With expert advice from Ian Cadlock,
Tenon Recovery*

Book Guild Publishing
Sussex, England

First published in Great Britain in 2007 by
The Book Guild Ltd
Pavilion View
19 New Road
Brighton, BN1 1UF

Typesetting in Times by
IML Typographers, Birkenhead, Merseyside

Printed in Great Britain by
CPI Bath

A catalogue record for this book is available from
The British Library.

ISBN 978 1 84624 168 0

For Wendy, Jack and Freddie,
John,
And for all those who fly a little too
close to the sun.

Contents

Preface   ix

Introduction   xiii

1   I Love This Game!   1

2   Catch Up   11

3   Life Is Our Most Valuable Asset   21

4   It's A Family Affair   31

5   Investments, Investments, Damned Investments   41

6   Buddy, Can You Spare A Dime?   51

7   The Net Closes In   61

8   A Night Of Triumph   71

9   One More Try   79

10   The End Is Just The Beginning   89

11   Straightforward Answers To All The Crucial Questions   97

12   Wendy's Way To Save A Wad   105

Epilogue   111

Appendix – Useful Contacts   115

Preface

Debt. The great unmentionable. The big no-no. The elephant in the room. According to the financial experts we are all up to our necks in the stuff – this year personal debt in the UK has exceeded £1.25* trillion, and it's rising fast: by £1 million every 3.85 minutes at the latest reckoning – so why is no one prepared to talk about it? Because debt is what happens to other people – right?

Well, not exactly – a staggering 6 million of us admit to struggling with our finances at any given time. Of these, 5,300 seek Citizens Advice Bureau help every day; one becomes insolvent every minute; and over 1.4 million are on the verge of bankruptcy. In short, we are a nation of over-spenders and serial consumers, buoyed up by a strong economy and seduced by a pervasive 'buy now, pay later' philosophy. There are now more credit cards in the UK than people, and almost 300 plastic transactions taking place every second to feed our habit. It is a sobering thought that this year alone banks and building societies will hand out £1 billion every day: the biggest ever home loan bonanza in Britain.

So what are the consequences of all this debt? According to a recent survey, over a third of British couples are

* All figures taken from *Credit Action*, Feb 2007

kept awake at night worrying about money, and a quarter of all of us who experience debt are receiving treatment for finance-related stress, anxiety or depression. There's even a fancy medical name for it: MSS (Money Sickness Syndrome). And still, three quarters of British couples find money the hardest subject of all to talk about!

With their glamorous lifestyle and *Hello* magazine credentials, TV star Gary Webster and his wife Wendy Turner (presenter of Channel 4's *Pet Rescue*) might seem the last people to fall into the trap of personal debt. The showbiz couple were, until recently, riding high on a wave of career success and personal triumph. They led a full, often extravagant life, making hay while the sun shines as their respective careers continued to flourish. Of course, like the rest of us, they had mortgages to pay, and families to support. But, while the going was good, the future could wait. Indefinitely! For Gary, as for many of us, the abiding motto was 'seize the day', and the devil-may-care star adopted an all-too-familiar 'ostrich' stance where prudent fiscal planning was concerned.

However, over the course of a single year (twelve months strewn with financial difficulties, family crises, terminated contracts, unforeseen tax bills, and, finally, the looming spectre of bankruptcy), Gary was to get a wake-up call that would make him re-evaluate his life. Like many other couples, Gary and Wendy were forced, for the first time, to face the facts of personal debt and all the heartache, indignity and logistical drama that comes with the territory.

Now, in this invaluable new book on personal debt and how to survive it, Gary Webster shares the stresses, strains, challenges and solutions that arose as a result of his spiralling insolvency. Part personal memoir, part self-help guide, *Debt Rescue* leads us through the minefield of personal debt and out the other side, drawing on Gary and Wendy's own experiences and the expert advice of financial recovery guru Ian Cadlock *en route*. That it does so with humour, lightness of touch and Gary's infectious optimism, makes *Debt Rescue* the perfect personal companion to recognising, negotiating and surviving your own money problems, whatever the scale. As personal debt in the UK continues to soar, *Debt Rescue* is a timely reminder that, where money matters are concerned, it's *always* good to talk.

Introduction

Financial woes are never easy to deal with at the best of times. For many they become all-consuming and can lead to anxiety, depression or even worse. Hopefully, in these pages you will find that there is light at the end of every tunnel and, however desperate a situation might get, it does, eventually, become easier. How do I know this? Because I've been through it. My philosophy on life has always been to see the good rather than the bad and if possible punctuate that with humour. I hope this book conveys some of that.

Although times have been tough, especially regarding my final day of destiny when I was declared bankrupt, I am always reminded to put those times into perspective by recalling the events that happened not three weeks later. Many lives were lost on and below London's streets in the tube and bus bombings of 7/7. As a Londoner myself I took this attack very personally and it served notice that whatever distress I was feeling it was nothing compared to the families and friends of those who had lost their lives simply travelling to work. Keeping things in perspective is a great asset when addressing your financial troubles. My attitude to the stress and hurt one has to deal with when one's cash flow is in freefall has been greatly helped by a fantastic network of friends and family who enjoy my comical take on all things, sometimes almost as much as I do.

Finally, when I was at my lowest and was closest to having the dreaded sleepless nights, two phrases would always spring into my head...

Your altitude is determined by your attitude.

If you think you can't you won't.

For many years I have tried to live by these fine words – to always strive and push myself and never to see any situation as insurmountable. These two phrases probably sum me up best. They were born from a man whom I've never met but admire greatly.

On 19 July 1989, Denny Fitch found himself assisting the pilot Al Haynes and his co-pilot on United Airlines flight 232 from Denver to Chicago. When the plane's hydraulic system suddenly failed Captain Haynes put out a call for assistance for Mr Fitch. Haynes knew that Fitch was on the plane and that with over 3,000 hours flying time on the DC10 he was one of United Airlines most accomplished and experienced pilots. The situation which Mr Fitch found himself confronted with was that the plane had become uncontrollable – it was like driving a car with no brakes and no steering. His determined goal against all odds was to get the plane down and all 285 passengers off safely. A landing strip in Sioux City, Iowa was designated as the only possible place for landing. Miraculously, Fitch put the plane onto the tarmac at Sioux City but tragically it proceeded to flip over, splitting into three parts and killing 100 passengers. However, due to the supreme flying skill of Denny Fitch and the other members of the cockpit, 185 people survived.

Mr Fitch remained in a coma for several days and upon coming round was distraught to learn that he had not saved all the passengers on board… his only thought was for others. The full extent of Fitch's skill and heroism can be quantified by the fact that in over one hundred simulated attempts, recreating the same conditions, no team of United Airlines pilots has ever been able to get the plane anywhere near to a position of landing.

When asked how he had done this Mr Fitch explained that, 'Your altitude is determined by your attitude'. His total belief that they were all going to make it somehow played a part in keeping the plane in the air. He went on to say, 'If you think you can't you won't'. In short, if he had doubted for one second they weren't all going to make it then none of them would have. In my mind he is a truly inspirational man and one whose words have always steered me on the right course when I've been in trouble.

In closing, I hope that this book can help others, inspire others and allow others to smile even in the toughest of times. It has been written to tell anyone who finds them-selves in a similar situation that you are not alone.

Enjoy.

1

I Love This Game

As I looked before me I had to rub my eyes once, twice and a third time. I wasn't dreaming. I *had* just seen contestant number 8, Miss Stockholm from Sweden, walk up and down the catwalk on one section of mile upon mile of beautiful white sand on Florida's world famous Daytona Beach. After contestant number 8 there were another 70 competitors to come. They had flown in from all over the world, striving to be crowned Miss Hawaiian Tropic 1993. I guess it was at this point, as the sun shone down and the sand was hot between my toes, that I turned to my best friend and partner in crime Phil Middlemiss and uttered the words that came in a somewhat trance-like state, 'I love this game…'

Phil, who will be referred to as Middo for most of this journey, slowly turned his head and, with beautiful understatement, replied (just as Miss Caracas walked by two feet above us), 'Do you? Do you really?'

Enough said. For many young actors *Hamlet* at The National would be the buzz, the pinnacle of the first five to ten years of a flourishing acting career. For me that is certainly something I would deeply love to do and would be honoured to experience. However, back then, at 28, having just completed the second series of the hit television series *Minder*, and being one of the two British TV stars invited to judge at the annual Hawaiian Tropic International Beauty Pageant, my Hamlets, my Macbeths and even my Juliets had all come at once. Middo and I were the guests of Ron Rice – owner and founder of the multi-million pound Hawaiian Tropic sun cream empire.

Although the trip itself was paid for, any extras such as booze, food, booze, excursions and… booze, were all down to Middo and me. But in such surroundings one tends to spend accordingly, and lack of generosity has never been one of my faults. So, my Plan A (of spending), never really had a Plan B to go along with it. If a party was to be had or a holiday enjoyed by me and everyone else then so be it. Unfortunately, or fortunately (whichever way you look at it) Middo was exactly the same, probably even more so. As two young, successful and popular actors we rather tended to bow down to the Viv Nicholson philosophy of financial management – Spend, Spend, Spend. The thought that the next series of *Minder* would be my last and I would not earn that kind of money again for another ten years never occurred to me. I was confident in my own ability and I thought that having landed the role of Ray Daley in *Minder*, a constant level of similarly well paid creative work would continue. The size of the rose-tinted glasses I had on must have been embarrassing. Oh why didn't anyone tell me? At that time it was simply not on my agenda to put money aside for a rainy day or to think about my future financial security and other clichés like that. My mission was to enjoy life to the full and to drag everyone with me. Big mistake looking back but great fun.

Anyway, let's not dwell on the past of parties, clubbing and forty-eight hour benders. Oh alright, just for a little while longer…

I guess one of the most memorable events I was asked to be involved with was the inaugural British Fashion Awards. As *Minder* was very much flavour of the month I was asked to present an award alongside Kylie Minogue. That's what I said, Kylie Minogue. Well, after I had rung my close friends, acquaintances and even my enemies with the news that I would be partying the night away with Kylie and the world's top supermodels, I suddenly experienced what all us girls do at a time like that – 'fashion panic'! What was I going to wear? This was in the days long before Trinny and Susannah, and my old stalwart Mister Byrites was not an option. Eventually I rolled with tradition in a bog standard dinner jacket.

So, there I was, well wadded up (that means lots of cash in pocket) for the evening's exploits, suited and booted and in the Green Room waiting to be introduced to Kylie. As I waited nervously, these legs, like tall pine trees, began to appear. It was only when I looked up that I realised they were attached to a body and then a head. I was in model country. I would like to tell you how beautiful Naomi, Claudia and Christy all were but I would have needed a set of ladders and a block and tackle to get anywhere near seeing their faces. If ever I needed some Cuban heels it was then. But my attention was soon taken as the PR girl came over to inform me that Kylie was on her way up and to run through what was expected of me. As she rambled on about where I was to walk on and off and what I was to say, all I could think about was Kylie. What would I say to her? Would my tongue engage with my mouth? Maybe we'd hit it off, get on well, dance the night away, have nightcaps back at my seventh floor two bedroom flat in Penge and end up making mad passionate love in every room (all four of them including the broom cupboard). All this until dawn when the morning sun would gently rise, and as it shone on Kylie's elfin face I would declare my undying love, tell her she could be so lucky, lucky, lucky, propose to her and be in all the Sunday newspapers on our honeymoon. And then I saw the vision; the vision that was six feet tall, dark and strikingly handsome in the shape of Kylie Minogue's pigging bastard boyfriend, Zane. She had a boyfriend – the one thing I hadn't bargained for. All I could hope was that the tension would build between ugly Zane and Kylie's ex, the late great Michael Hutchence. Yes, he was there too and in full rock star garb – ripped jeans, leather jacket and shades and canoodling with his latest squeeze Helena Christiansen in another corner of the increasingly beautiful Green Room.

Unfortunately the battle of the beautiful people didn't materialise but I still had a truly memorable evening on Boy George's table alongside Kylie and Zane and any number of blondes, brunettes and redheads. A heavy smoker at the time, I lived off the story of George and Kylie and Christy cadging the occasional fag off me as the night drifted into the morning for several weeks. The story was cemented when a couple of months later Middo and I went, as personally invited guests, to the Kylie concert at the Manchester Apollo. Summoned to see Kylie before the show, Middo and I knocked on her door with some trepidation, only to be greeted by a beaming Kylie thrusting a packet of twenty Silk Cut into my hand with the inscription 'Thanks, Love Kylie' on the cellophane. A true star with true star quality. That packet was my holy grail for many years until one seriously heavy drinking session when, too lazy to go to the shops, I ripped open the packet for my nicotine rush, and now, alas, the famous Kylie-signed fag packet has gone forever.

But let's get back to one final peek at Hawaiian Tropic... we were invited guests of Ron Rice, primarily due to the fact that the *Sunday Mirror* was covering our trip, and it would be great publicity for Hawaiian Tropic sun cream in the UK. Some of the sights we saw over our week of bliss were quite extraordinary – the most revealing being that of Ron Rice's décor in his Daytona Beach mansion. Think footballers wives meets Jade Goody and you'll get some sort of picture of what I am talking about. Alongside the Barbara Cartland touches there were items dotted around the house that bore no relation to man or beast. There was a stuffed full-sized, authentic, killer lion that looked out over the sea from his living room. Shot and killed in Africa, the lion was supposed to have eaten fifteen villagers over a two year period before being eventually slain by a paid hunter. Now it was stuffed and mounted and owned by Ron. Perhaps this is what I should have been saving my money for... not! But far and away the *pièce de resistance* was slap bang in the middle of his lounge. There in its full glory was a full-sized 24 carat gold-plated common-or-garden dustbin. Why? You may ask. We did. So here goes... back in the sixties when Ron was dropping out of college in California he had time on

5

his hands. And to help with his finances he would mix together a few lotions and potions, a bit of aloe vera here and there, a dash of coconut and a never revealed secret ingredient – all in said dustbin. From his garage he would sell the cool, smooth and sweet smelling sun cream at ten cents a bottle and I'm sure you can guess the rest. From these humble beginnings Ron's mighty empire was born. And just as a reminder that the true American Dream can be lived, Ron gold-plated the very dustbin from which it all started, and plonked it, as bold as brass (or gold in Ron's case) in the middle of his living room. So so *so* American, but a decent chap and a fantastic host… in a Heffner kind of way. But that's another story for my autobiography when I'm a hundred percent sure I'm on my death bed.

To live in that kind of company one tends to spend like that kind of company and what should have been a freebie trip turned out to be anything but. Still, buying the Miss Stockholm and Miss Angelholm sashes off the two respective Swedish contestants (when I say buy, I mean taking them for a champagne soaked meal at Daytona's best restaurant) was worth every penny. By returning home with the sashes in our suitcases, that one act of ridiculous expenditure put me and Middo into legend status amongst our friends. Maybe that's where my philosophy has always been wrong – to live for the moment and enjoy to the max – rather than just once take a step back and assess the situation through rational eyes. Those rose-tinted spectacles must have been welded to the bridge of my nose! It's only now that I can see how pounds that were frittered away could have been put to so much better use.

Well, that's some of my history and in the next section we'll see how that history eventually caught up with me and the financial nightmare began to slowly unfold.

WHAT RAINY DAY ?

Webbo's Expert Advice on How to Avoid the 'Hawaiian Tropic' Effect

The sun may be shining now but we could have a hurricane tomorrow…

Make sure you save money for when you are out of work. Investments such as premium bonds are a good bet. It is not wise to play the stock markets with money you can't afford to lose.

Like Miss Caracas – You can look but you can't touch!

As a freelance worker you have to realise that a certain percentage of the money you have been paid is not actually yours and must one day leave your account to go to the tax man. You may look at it longingly but you must not spend it!

Sand in your privates must be dealt with straightaway…

When sand gets into all those creases and crevices, you must deal with it straightaway lest it stay there and fester. The same principles must apply to your finances – post, bills, VAT returns etc. – lest they come back to haunt you at a later date.

2

Catch Up

I guess one of the hardest things to tell anyone who is young and enjoying life is to stop enjoying it. And as nobody told me, I didn't. Looking back there were signs telling me but I, like the great Lionel Richie song says, 'was too blind to see'. The first of these occurred in November 2000, just 18 months after my wedding to the love of my life, TV presenter Wendy Turner. In keeping with my penchant for spending, the wedding was a quiet private affair with just 350 of our closest friends awaiting our arrival at the main hall of The Park Lane Hotel. This was after we had just had our nuptials tied at the Marie Antoinette Suite at The Ritz Hotel. Yes, we are talking Park Lane and we are talking The Ritz, London.

Thinking back now, the first sign I was definitely heading for trouble was at that very wedding. Sometimes when you meet your life partner they are somewhat different to you. Although they might laugh at your jokes and enjoy the same films and indulge in similar sexual practices (you haven't lived until you've been smothered in tofu and doused in hoisin sauce), usually relationships are like a positive and negative. If one is wild the other is calm. One mad, the other sane. One spends, one saves. It was on one particular night in The Ritz prior to our date of destiny that I realised Wendy was Gary and vice versa. I distinctly remember drunkenly arguing with Wendy until the wee small hours about the benefits of having the house champagne rather than the Dom Perignon she had earlier ordered for our 60 odd guests at the Marie Antoinette Suite. I explained that my Aunty Iris and my dear mother wouldn't know the difference between champagne, pomagne or alka seltzer, and that we would probably be wasting our booty from *OK!* magazine when we could use that moola on inviting another guest. Finally, I rang The Ritz to tell them that contrary to the previous night's demands, the Dom would now be replaced by the 'ouse.

On our wedding night, every penny of the £80,000 that *OK!* paid us for the rights to photograph our marriage was spent. Nobody paid for a thing and no one went dry, and everyone who we held dear and wanted to be there came. Another sign I guess. But people have always come before money in my book. And after seeing Wendy's love of the finer things during that period, I knew we were two peas in a pod that sooner or later, due to financial mismanagement, would go 'pop'.

So, 18 months after that, family life was full steam ahead. Jack, our adorable first son had recently celebrated his first birthday, and due to my lack of work I was happily performing my task of house husbandry. Wendy was working feverishly on her very popular TV series, *Pet Rescue*, and that meant on any given week being away for two or more days. During this time Jack and I built up a very secure and loving relationship, one that I also have with our second son, the equally adorable if slightly more crazy Freddie. Although there was much enjoyment looking after Jack, my income input was zilch and there had been a growing interest from the Inland Revenue about two or three previous years' tax returns and payments that had not been submitted. I was still on the roll that 'something would come up'. It always did. The pile of brown envelopes had started to build. I say envelopes because they remained unopened. But they could wait. I was happy looking after Jack and looking forward to this particular Thursday when I was going over to the Paxton Arms – a pub from my previous abode at Crystal Palace. No disrespect to Jack but I was starved of some adult company and a pint of Nelson Mandela (Stella) and a discussion on the merits of a 4,4,2 system or whether Arsene should sell or keep Patrick Vieira was always appealing.

Twenty-four hours later, having sat up all night and much of the next day drinking and bemoaning my fate to my pals at the pub, I returned home and of course, quite rightly, straight into the dog house. On my way back, the rain had started to fall and night was creeping in, compounding the guilt of my lateness. Wendy opened the door to a rather damp husband and sat for 15 minutes listening to my apologies, though with a wry smile, knowing that she wouldn't have minded a drink herself. It was at this point a knock came at the door and I unsteadily rose to answer it. At the very least it was a diversion from my present predicament. On opening the door I was asked the question, 'Gary Webster?'

'Yes,' I replied.

'Gary Ian Webster, 33 Ailsa Avenue?'

'Right again,' I replied. 'You're getting good at this.'

'I know,' he said. 'Royal Courts of Justice petition for unpaid taxes served. How good is that?'

I immediately hit back with my razor sharp wit, 'Fuck off, you bastard!'

'I'll be back!' was the cry as an envelope was thrust at me and the perpetrator left into the darkness.

Through blurred eyes I opened the envelope. The information was perfectly clear. A court date had been set for a bankruptcy hearing within six weeks for the sum of £25,000 in unpaid income tax. Unless paid in full, a petition of bankruptcy would be served. At that point I realised that life was going to get a lot tougher. What I didn't realise was that this was the start of a long financial struggle that five years later would indeed culminate in me being declared bankrupt.

I handed the letter to Wendy and walked outside into the pouring rain. I looked to the heavens and shouted, 'Why me? *Why me?*' If it hadn't been for the highly emotional charged state I was in due to the copious amounts of alcohol I had consumed over the last 24 hours I would have known exactly *why me*. My 'live today, worry later' lifestyle had caught up with me – a philosophy that will most certainly flounder if one doesn't have a weekly wage to back it up. I was a loving dad and husband but I had no job, no savings and certainly no desire to burden Wendy with a predicament of my own making. I had to find

£25,000 over the next six weeks or else I was going to be shamed into bankruptcy. What was I to do? Who could I turn to? Where could I go? The answer, as any red-blooded, independent male of the 21st century will tell you, was easy… my mum.

I made arrangements with an office I had not spoken to since 'gay' meant being generally happy (i.e. the Inland Revenue), to the effect that if I could pay the £25,000 in full before February 2001 then the bankruptcy petition would be rescinded and life would go back to normal. Or that's what I thought. So, having just six weeks to find £25,000, I set about broaching the subject with my mum to borrow the money to pay off the full amount. With great trepidation I sat my mum down and explained the situation – that her being of independent means and with no mortgage on her family home, she could help me out of the shit. With her razor sharp Essex wit she responded, 'Fuck off, you bastard.' But after some serious begging, we decided to take the option of raising the money by remortgaging her house to the tune of £25,000 with me paying the monthly repayments. This scheme has, in actual fact, worked very well to this day. Although the remortgage is in my mother's name, all the payments have been made by me. Well, nearly all, but that's another story. This is a good pointer to anyone in this situation that has access to someone else who can remortgage and has the sort of trusting relationship that only a mother and son can have. My mum and I are at present still not speaking. Only joking! The old coot rings me every time the payment's late.

The £25,000 was subsequently paid and the petition was withdrawn, and that I thought, was the end of the matter. This was not to be the case. As my excellent accountant Bill Shaw had always stressed to me, each year should be dealt with at the time. But as usual, due to my incompetence, I had certainly let things lapse. Thus, the realisation that the time it takes for the Inland Revenue to finally serve a bankruptcy petition might take several years from the year in question. The £25,000 I had just paid was from the combined years of '95, '96 and '97 so I was not in the clear or up to date at all. I was in catch up.

In catch up, but with no work, a large overdraft and a repayment scheme with my mum to honour. I knew that for the years '98, '99 and 2000 a similar amount to that I had just paid out would be needed. I had to find work and soon to stop a repeat of the nightmare I had just gone through.

Looking back, I feel if I had gone bankrupt then it would have saved a whole lot of trouble for the future. All my tax liabilities up to 2001 would have been struck off. I could then have started from scratch and been more diligent and responsible from that day on putting 40% of my earnings away for tax and 17.5% for VAT. By 'away' I mean into a separate untouchable account only to become active at the end of every tax year. With no credit cards to worry about I would have to live and make do with what was left. I guess ignoring the bankruptcy option at this time was down to a number of things: the embarrassment and stigma, which, until you have been made bankrupt, you assume goes with the territory; the sense of failure and perhaps more than anything, this disappointment that I could not do enough to pull myself out of the situation. The failure; disappointment and shame myths I was of course to realise later are created by the people who have no idea what bankruptcy is like. I shall highlight these ridiculous notions in later sections. For now, I knew that the storm was over but the hurricane was gathering pace.

Webbo's Expert Advice on the 'Dom Perignon' Effect

Harsh reality can lead to strained relations

Don't feel belittled or have your nose put out of joint if those who are lending you money want to cover their backs. With my mum, she insisted (quite rightly) that a solicitor dealt with the remortgaging of her property. A legally binding contract was drawn up and I was honour bound to keep up the repayments on my mum's account. Even if, as it happened, I went bankrupt, my mum would then be treated like any other creditor and would seek to be fully compensated. This is only right as it keeps the loan structured and is beneficial to all in the long run. The biggest reason for family fallouts is money – beware!

Overnight success can take many years

Once confronted with your first financial scare, ensure that you make no other monetary commitments and plan your finances better from that day on. Do not assume anything regarding work or improved wages as they may never come. Act swiftly to get things straightened out.

If in doubt, bust out

If the future looks very bleak indeed, then it could be the best option to go bankrupt at the first opportunity, but make sure that you are prepared for it. Be ready to function with a strict and ordered fiscal attitude. It will be tough at the time but you may reap the benefits in the years to come rather than be beset by constant worries.

Financial recovery guru Ian Cadlock says

By the time Gary was made bankrupt, he would have received – and ignored – many documents demanding payment. There are two vital tips here:

1. Always read or listen to any creditor pressure, however much you'd rather not.

2. Always respond: you will need goodwill from your creditors and the best way to lose it is to ignore them.

3

Life Is Our Most Valuable Asset

Things at the beginning of June 2004 weren't going too badly at all. I'd been playing the character of Gary Costello, a family man and all round good guy, in Channel 5's flagship soap opera *Family Affairs* for eleven months. My career and finances seemed to be, for the first time in a long time, under control. Although I knew that large tax bills were still looming from previous years, the thought did not particularly worry me as I was working and the prospects looked good. The storylines and the performances involving the Costello family had been nominated for two British Soap Awards, which we narrowly missed out on in May 2004. As we know, *Family Affairs* is a soap and unless you're 'crap in the sun' (a.k.a. *Eldorado*) or 'crap in the Midlands' (a.k.a. *Crossroads*) or 'fucking crap anywhere you like' (a.k.a. *Albion Market*) soaps just don't get axed, do they?

Things were stable and, as I said, I knew bills were on their way, so with that in mind I decided to head the enemy off at the pass – fight fire with fire, make a pre-emptive strike against the dictator of the Inland Revenue and his BMDs (Bills of Mass Destruction). I bought a flat in Richmond with the idea of doing it up and thus selling it at a profit. Then I would be ready to pay off any demands that came my way. I sat back and wondered in awe at my great idea, probably in the same way Clive Sinclair did over his C5. I had made the fatal mistake of now giving myself two hefty mortgages a month to pay. I was earning good money, but not that good, and once again had failed to put aside the one commodity that had caused me so much trouble over the last ten years – beer money. No, my tax. Whether or not the flat scheme worked will be revealed in a later section, but as I said, at the beginning of June 2004 things weren't going too badly at all.

The weekend of 25 June 2004 had started somewhat chaotically, but that is the norm in the Webster household. The whole family, which now numbered four with the birth of little Freddie in 2003, were all up at Wendy's parents' house dog-sitting. Her mum and dad were on their customary holiday abroad – a surprise destination Christmas present that Wendy gave them every year. This year it was Madeira, a long time favourite with Wendy's mum due to its fine climate, and her penchant for getting tiddly on the stuff. After waving goodbye to them on Friday we were all looking forward to a week of fun. As I was only up for the weekend due to my *Family Affairs* commitments (I had to be back at work on Tuesday morning), and as Freddie was at his crawling best, another pair of hands was needed. And who are you going to call when the chips are down? You guessed it – mum! Again!

So, everything was sorted. Over the hot and humid weekend Wendy was away at a horse show and the boys and I had been having great adventures in Nono and Pop's garden and at the local Waterworld Park. Nanny Kathleen (a.k.a. my mum) had been asleep. At the end of Sunday night we were all pretty tired and, certainly for Wendy, the weekend's exertions were beginning to show. A stiff neck and headache and general flu-like symptoms were dragging her down. So much so that a trip to the walk-in clinic on Sunday night was duly taken. Armed with some strong painkillers and a diagnosis of summer flu, 'two every fours hours and a good night's sleep' was the prognosis.

Setting off on Monday afternoon with Wendy feeling a little better but still not a hundred per cent, I was hoping that another good night's sleep would do the trick and Tuesday morning would bring an end to it. For Wendy, the respite was short lived. Waking on Tuesday, if anything a hundred per cent worse, she managed to drag herself to her local GP to plead her case. 'Everyone has headaches', was the medical advice she received. Totally ignoring this somewhat condescending advice, she set about ordering a taxi to the North Staffordshire Royal Infirmary. My wife's sixth sense is born out of experience – she has been on the sharp end of Malaria, double pneumonia (twice), single pneumonia (three times), and pleurisy in the space of her 35 years – and she knew all was not well in the state of Stoke. Taking Jack as ballast and leaving Nanny Kathleen (now thankfully awake) with Freddie, she set off for the hospital.

After a long and train-delayed journey on Monday night I had a match-stick-propping-up-the-eye-lids call time for work the next morning. Fortunately my work was over by lunchtime, making it the kind of day I really like.

Knowing that Wendy was going to the doctor's that morning, I was awaiting her call when I had stripped off my shirt and was in the process of removing my trousers to prepare for an afternoon lounging around on the sofa. When I shuffled, Chaplinesque, trousers round my ankles, to the phone, little did I know that my perspective on life was to change once again. It was not Wendy updating me on the news of her ailments but Nanny Kathleen with the news that, whilst she was ensconced with one child under three, two dogs, three cats, and a washing machine on the blink, Wendy had collapsed at the hospital with suspected meningitis.

In my life, I have only ever received one other call with such devastating news. And with the greatest irony, I also received that news, the news of my father's death, with my trousers around my ankles – my brother being the harbinger of death as I shuffled (this time from the toilet) to the phone. Believe me, I have now adopted a completely different style to my relaxation and never, but never answer, the phone when visiting the room of contemplation.

Meningitis is such a dirty word. Like cancer, it is dark immediately, a gathering storm. Some disease-associated words carry with them a sort of optimism, even though they are life threatening. My father had two heart attacks and survived; Wendy had pneumonia and did the same. But words like leukaemia, haemorrhage and meningitis always seem to have a thick suffocating cloud that surrounds them; a smell of pessimism, a sense of death. And now Wendy had collapsed with suspected meningitis.

24

The many thoughts that raced through my mind on what seemed like a never-ending train journey to Stoke-on-Trent are a blur to me now. But the cloud never left me. I felt like the cartoon character that is constantly followed by his own individual cloud burst, raining down on him.

As I approached Intensive Care I was met by Wendy's Aunty Marguerite who had come to look after Jack. She pointed me in the direction of Wendy's room. I was met by a scene, which mirrored an old master's painting. There, sitting outside the room, was my son Jack, upright, concentrated and strong, like a guardian angel protecting the room from any ill. He turned instinctively and ran to me, upon which he received the biggest hug the proudest daddy could ever give. As we walked into Wendy's room and I saw my frail, vulnerable wife asleep, I knew that whatever was coming our way, whatever roller-coaster ride of ups and downs was going to befall us in the future, my only wish was for us to experience them together and that life itself was all that mattered. Nothing would ever be insurmountable, nothing would ever be so important, no stress or pressure would ever get on top of us. As long as Wendy pulled through, then we had already succeeded.

One's spending habits and one's responsibility to contain them are not always a simple case of a lack of understanding or respect. Like many major things that happen to us in life it is usually a collection of minor things that lead to the end product. Seeing my wife lying so ill in that hospital bed confirmed my resolve to never let anything that wasn't life threatening get on top of me. Some dozen years earlier the death of my father had resulted in my thought

25

patterns moving in a completely different direction: his death had fuelled my 'live today, worry later' attitude. My view on mortality had been shaken. A 'what's the point?' attitude had arisen. If it didn't go right, if the work stopped, if the money ran out, would I care? I had just lost my dad. He had been extremely supportive at the early part of my career and now he was going to miss the pay off, the punch line, and it wasn't fair. Looking back, for quite a few years that was my excuse for living on the edge. Eventually that manifestation of grief passes and one is inspired by marriage and children, and ultimately work. It is then that one realises that one cannot continue to live without responsibility and asks, 'Where did it all go?'

So now I have gone from looking to the heavens and asking my dad to somehow inform me on the mysteries of life, to the more simple request of the six Lotto numbers every Saturday night. Needless to say, neither have ever been forthcoming. I think he would have liked it that way.

The next 48 hours, as Wendy lay very ill but conscious, were as long as any I can remember, and that includes a weekend bender with Middo in Galway one summer. After being informed by the specialist looking after Wendy that we would have to wait 24 hours for the results of a painful lumbar puncture to determine whether she had contracted the extremely serious viral meningitis or the more fatal bacterial meningitis, I set off to call the *Family Affairs* office to explain the situation. If Wendy had the highly contagious bacterial meningitis, then Jack, Freddie and I would all be put in quarantine. When I told the production scheduler I wouldn't be in the next day as I had had to rush up to Stoke to see my sick wife, her immediate reaction was priceless. 'Are you sure? Well we can't change the schedule, you'll have to get back.' When I explained that if the tests showed up bacterial meningitis and that I could be a potential carrier, and theoretically infect the whole show, I was greeted with, 'Stay as long as you need to! Whatever it takes! And give our love to your lovely wife, Wanda.' Ah, the caring nature of show business never ceases to amaze me.

Thankfully, if thankfully is the right word, the tests came back showing viral meningitis and the next thing was for Wendy to be pumped full of anti-viral drugs and to spend the next ten days in the infectious diseases wing of the hospital. For Wendy, the omens were good as she was given the same bed in the IDW as she was when she had Malaria some years before. A nice touch, I thought, albeit with rubber gloves on. After spending three months in Stoke-on-Trent convalescing at Nono and Pop's house, it took Wendy over a year to finally shake off the recurring headaches and extreme fatigue. I knew that Wendy was back to full strength when we got particularly drunk one night and she woke up with no ill effects. But by that time I had been declared bankrupt. It seems a strange dichotomy to be declared bankrupt but celebrating with your wife. But this is how I felt after remembering Wendy on her hospital bed, for I knew that it was life and not money that was our most precious asset.

Webbo's Expert Guide to Survival

Second opinions could mean second chances

Never be afraid to ask for a second opinion. If your body doesn't feel right, go back to the doctor until it does. The NHS staff, doctors and nurses do a fantastic job but they are overworked and human. Like any of us, they can make mistakes. Don't be afraid to ask again – it could save your life. Likewise, if you find yourself in financial strife don't accept the first verdict. Get a second, third, fourth opinion and give yourself a second chance.

Infectious diseases rule OK

All the money in the world means nothing unless you can spend it with those you love. Sometimes it takes a major, even life threatening event for one to appreciate that. Remember, however bad your financial woes might seem, put them in perspective and remind yourself of what really matters.

Never answer a ringing phone

If you ever find yourself on the seat of 'quiet thinking' and the phone's ringing, let it ring. There is nothing less dignified than hearing bad news in a compromising position. But also, there is nothing more human than having to deal with the basics of life before moving on. Take time to contemplate and be prepared for whatever life decides to throw at you and then approach it head on… preferably with your trousers up!

4

It's A Family Affair

Working on any sort of television programme can be intensive, time consuming and stressful at the best of times. Working on a soap is something else. Of course, as I always tried to impress upon my fellow actors, it was hard, but it wasn't nursing or teaching. Hard work aside, it was immensely enjoyable and the pros far outweighed the cons. The intensity of working on a soap naturally lends itself to a camaraderie and a family feeling that one is unlikely to experience anywhere else in the field of entertainment. By the word on the street and from fellow actors, *Family Affairs* had by far and away the most punishing schedule in the business and it was nothing to complete 60 or 70 pages of dialogue in a 14 hour day. With that sort of work load, play time between the cast and crew was also of a high intensity. *Family Affairs* became legendary for its work hard, party hard ethos, a reputation that continued right up to its demise. Tickets for its end of series party were more sought after than Britney Spears' web site and rarer than rocking horse shit. For me, running parallel to the heavy work load, was my fight for financial survival...

As the squeeze from the Customs and Excise and Inland Revenue departments began to take effect, so my need to raise money to keep the wolves from the door began to crank up to fever pitch. For many actors the quiet and solace of their dressing-room in between scenes and at lunchtime is their sanctuary. For me, it was where some of my best work was done as my desperate attempts to gain a loan, placate my creditors and stave off bankruptcy was becoming my own real life drama. On many occasions, having dealt with a radio rental (mental) wife, a missing daughter, a shop-lifting minor and a philandering mother on set, off set I would have to deal with the likes of Picture A Loan or Norton Finance to ask why my loan application had been turned down.

As an avid Arsenal fan, one of the frequent conversations I had with the producers of the show was that I could deal with the fact that my wife had faked our daughter's cancer, I could handle that our eldest daughter was having an affair with the local rapist, that even my mother was shagging my best mate in our basement, but to make my character a West Ham fan, now that was really taking the proverbial biscuit. So whilst all this was happening on set, in my dressing-room I set about the task in hand. Now is a good time to point out that all that glitters is not gold. What the numerous TV and newspaper adverts for loan companies offer, and what they actually deliver, are two entirely different things. In Chapter 5 we will go into detail about the loan companies and highlight the main anomalies that can be found in their promises.

Meanwhile, back on set, the one incident that I think best defines my struggle to juggle work and potential financial ruin came just before Christmas 2004. Working on a groundbreaking and extremely well written story-line involving paedophilia, the days were very long and intensive. The story-line was treated with the highest care and respect by everyone involved, from the series producer to the actors and crew. The outline of the story was that a young, close family friend was discovered to be sexually abusing our youngest daughter. This subject had been blanked by every other soap but due to the courage and compassion of the *Family Affairs* production they had decided to run it to highlight that this type of abuse is happening today.

My focus was also being swamped by constant phone calls from the Customs and Excise regarding my ever mounting VAT debt. These phone calls took on a more serious edge when a secondary demand, amounting to an 'immediately payable' £6,500, landed on my doorstep. This money was born out of outstanding debt from many years before, and after speaking to my accountant, we realised that it had to be settled without further ado as it was basically serving as a bail bond for any further outstanding debts that would inevitably arise. Failure to pay this money, like failure to secure bail in a court case, could result in imprisonment. But, as I say, it was not life or death. My accountant and I set about allaying the VAT operative's fears, and after a few desperate phone calls we came to an arrangement to try and settle the problem in early January 2005.

Unfortunately, because of the farce that is bureaucracy in the multi-conglomerate departments of officialdom, the matter had already been passed on to the obligatory debt collecting agency. I duly realised this when a threatening demand for the money by a certified thug agency (I mean the bailiffs) arrived on my doormat. Not wanting to worry Wendy, and knowing that to a certain extent the matter was in hand, I faxed Bill, my accountant, the said demand for him to deal with. The only access I had to a fax machine was at the production office at work. Ah, there's the rub. Having quietly gone into the said production office and set about faxing the letter across, I realised that all was not right. I slyly asked for advice, not wanting to show exactly what I was sending. Up to now, all my financial woes had been kept secret from those at work. Embarrassment was still rearing its ugly head and it was something I just didn't want the whole world to know. I was told that I had to dial '9' to get an outside line and I merrily went about my business, safe in the knowledge that Bill had received the fax and would now be setting about telling the bailiffs to back off.

My very rare lunchtime nap was interrupted by a firm, but not loud, knock, the sort that policemen or TV licence inspectors make. A knock with a quiet authority, which in my experience always spells trouble. It was Alison Davis, our series producer with whom I had a great relationship: I was therefore puzzled at the inference of the knock. She asked me if I had recently sent a fax. Stunned, I replied that I had at which point she handed me a faxed copy of my original document. My mind and heart were racing; not why, not where, not who, just *how? How? How?* Alison quickly explained that she had no interest in the private fax (yeah, right – I had visions of her leaving my dressing-room shouting, 'Hey everybody, keep it to yourself but Webbo's gone tits up!'). However, it had come into her possession via *Talk Back Thames*' then Head of Drama Paul Marquess's secretary. Still non-plussed, she reiterated that it had come through on his internal fax machine. Now, to say Paul was high up on the food chain is an understatement. After Peter Fincham, the Chairman, he *was* the food chain. Due to my ignorance of all things technical, having not dialled a '9' for an outside line at my first attempt to send the fax, it had arrived at the Head of Drama's fax machine. This is the kind of luck one has when one is being flushed down the toilet. My bad luck was compounded by the fact that pretty soon contract renegotiations were about to start and my bargaining power had just dropped by at least 100 points on the FTSE.

Alison left the matter with me and I had that sinking feeling that even a cracking episode of *Neighbours* couldn't get me out of. There was only one thing for it – to go out that night and get 'Duffetted'. And what, you might ask, is to get Duffetted? The noun is Nicola and the verb is to Duffett. Nicola Duffett was, and still is, a legend in theatrical circles. Best remembered for her roles in *Eastenders* and as Cat in *Family Affairs*, Nicola has also graced stage and screen in the West End and under the tutelage of Merchant and Ivory. Her CV speaks for itself but what is never written about is her *joie de vivre*: she is one of the best party-goers I have ever had the good fortune to share a drink with.

On first arriving on *Family Affairs*, Nicola would always be the first to meet and greet and make one feel welcome. This would usually take the form of a good week's work followed by a drink at the local pub on a Friday. For most of us that would be it, but not for Nicola. Her staying power is unique and after my first experience of a welcome to the FA family (we started drinking on Friday afternoon and I finally left Nicola's with the party still going on Saturday evening), I christened the phrase 'I've been Duffetted'. Believe me, getting out on Saturday evening was a result. Subsequently, over my two and a half years at *Family Affairs*, my Duffettings have been numerous. It was always fun to see a new member of the cast roll in on a Monday morning, deathly white, drawn and zombie like. Lying in darkness in their dressing-room, a barely human nod would be their reply to my question, 'Duffetted?'

Obviously, as my financial situation moved into melt-down, my Duffettings decreased. It was always with a great sense of relief that upon seeing some other poor bastard on the said Monday morning, one could say, 'Thank God it's not me!' But as I explained, after the fax incident there was only one thing for it – 'when in doubt, get Duffetted out!'

Webbo's Expert View on Getting Hammered

You are only as good as your last job

Always enjoy every job you do as it may be your last for a little while. As with the acting profession, any job is hard work, but hopefully rewarding. Keep focused on the rewarding bits. If there aren't any, never be afraid to take a leap of faith and try something new. It could change your life as well as your bank balance.

I wish I'd listened to my dad more

Try to have some basic knowledge on all things electrical and of the 21st century. I tended to switch off when being shown how to wire a plug or change a light bulb by my dad. Subsequently I missed the fax-sending lesson too. This applies equally to finance. Knowledge is power, so flex those brain muscles and arm yourself with all the facts at your disposal. It could save your bacon in the long run!

I always thought I went a Duffett too far

Know when to stop partying and have enough brain cells left to tell the story. Your problems cannot be hidden behind a state of inebriation. Things may be tough but will definitely be easier to deal with in the cold, *sober* light of day.

Financial recovery guru Ian Cadlock says

Communicate! Letting people know what is going on will alleviate your anxiety, and everyone concerned – even the Revenue and Customs – will try to help if they are aware of your problems.

5

Investments, Investments, Damned Investments

How many times as an unemployed actor, during the late nineties and early noughties, had I seen the numerous daytime advertisements for loan and remortgaging companies? The proliferation of these ads has coincided with the increase of personal debt. Subsequently the tone of the adverts has subtly changed. Gone is the encouragement to free up your cash from your house in order to enjoy the pleasures of life, i.e. a car, holiday or celebration. No, the need to have access to cash via a remortgage or a loan is to pay off your debts, which have accrued in an ever more unstable financial market. With that as a base the promises become grander but the small print becomes microscopic. And as any good financial advisor will tell you, always read the small print!

As the VAT and income tax letters began to pile up, my options were becoming limited. One was to invest, to make a quick buck, to speculate to accumulate, and pay off what was owed and start again. The other was to borrow and pay off what was owed but continue to pay for it for some 25 years. In late 2003 I decided, or rather Wendy and I decided, to plump for the first option. Using money Wendy had put aside for her own income tax bill due at the end of tax year 2005, we put down a deposit on

41

a three-bedroom flat in the exclusive area of Richmond Hill.

The flat was for sale at a very good price – you know, elderly couple have moved out (OK, died), one vicar owner, that kind of thing. Our plan was to sell it on at a huge profit after a total refurbishment. Putting down a £25,000 deposit, we got a mortgage in my name for £250,000. Ours was a three-bedroom flat and the two-bedroom flats in the same block were already going for £340,000. The market was booming! With a new kitchen, a new bathroom, new carpets, repainting throughout, and at a total outlay of £15,000, we could put it on the market for around £365,000 and our troubles would be over. That's right, our troubles would be over! A clear profit at a pessimistic estimate would be £50,000. I would then make a generous offer to the VAT man (which I was confident he would accept, having had nothing from me for the past year). Wendy would get her money back and my shoulders would be less hunched. Yes, our troubles would be over!

Looking back, if only I had seen the power of the meningitis bug, a delay in renovations and of course, what Tony and Gordon promised us would never happen – a bust in the housing market. 'A slow down in the market is occurring,' they said. It was more like investing in Betamax. 'The market's gone quiet.' Like a fucking library! And a reversal of fortune Claus Von Bülow would have been proud of! We came so close, but as always, that is when the hard work really begins. So, as we watched any projected profit slowly dwindle and our asking price come down at a rate of knots the dinosaur-destroying meteorite would have been happy with, we realised that the answer to our financial prayers was fast becoming less and less viable.

The flat became a huge financial burden, with a monthly outlay of £1,600 and nothing to show for it. Surely our investment in property was as safe as, well, houses? I think the lessons one learns from this experience is that buying a second property for a tidy financial profit must only be done with a long-term aim in mind. The market can not always be guaranteed over a short-term timescale. If you look at is as a pension plan, however, say over 20 to 25 years, the chances are that you will come out of it OK. I hadn't realised that like any game of chance the housing market can be a big gamble when you try and turn a quick profit.

Having seen option one blow or rather begin to fizzle out, my mind turned to what I was being bombarded with every day, five days a week. *'Need a loan? Then look no further! Secured or unsecured, just give us a ring!'* Yes, I was about to sell my soul to the Devil but my time was running short and anyway *Dr Faustus* had always been one of my favourite plays. What you must realise when you push the final digit on your phone that puts you through to one of these loan companies is that you are theirs for life and will become immensely popular for a while, with people ringing you at all times of day or night inquiring if you have indeed secured your loan yet. My first call was to Norton Finance – a choice based on nothing more than the fact that Wendy comes from a village called Norton in Stoke-on-Trent! As the questions rolled in from a very cheery young man my fears began to wash away and I really began to think that what these companies promised was true.

Are you working? Yes.

Annual salary? After tax (well, after I got around to paying it) about 50K.

Home owner? Yes, a three-bedroom flat on Richmond Hill.

Mortgage? Yes, £250,000, and it's worth at least £350,000! (Of course, I didn't tell them that the price was going down quicker than a German porn star.)

And then the big one… *How much are you looking to borrow, Mr Webster?*

Being new to the game, I thought I'd go with what we thought we could at least make from the sale of the flat to get ourselves into the clear and I said boldly, '£50,000.' Much to my delight and disbelief he didn't drop the phone or even cough in a way that suggested he had put his hand over the receiver and was now in tears of laughter with his co-workers in their airless office. Instead the reply came, '£50,000? That should be fine, Mr Webster! I shall now give all your information to our financial team and they will ring you with confirmation of your loan within the next forty-eight hours.'

Could this be true? Did my ears deceive me? Had he really

said *confirmation of my loan?* He had! I had ticked all the boxes and it was a goer!

'Will there be anything else, sir?' the now wonderfully cheery Paul or Steve or Michael or whatever his name was asked.

Filled with unbridled glee I quipped 'Yes, another £50,000 please!' Oh, how we laughed. I put the phone down and for the first time in ages I really felt that things were beginning to look up. The air was good, the birds were singing and I had a spring in my step. Well, that's not exactly true. Freddie was crying as he had just done a stinky poo and before I could get to him he undid his own nappy and proceeded to mount a one-man dirty cell protest. But still, life was on the up. forty-eight hours… just two short days before having a cheque for £50,000. We could pay off some of the debts and breath easy again. I was in regular work. We could sell the flat straight away for a tidy but small profit and ditch the second mortgage of £1,600 a month coming out of my dwindling salary. In short, it would be a godsend. But alas, as many of you reading this who are in a similar situation will know, it just doesn't go according to plan when you're in the shit. It's a bit like a football club struggling against relegation. You just don't seem to get the rub of the green: penalties against rather than for, a ball that crosses the line but was not seen by the ref, and the classic last-minute mistake rather than a piece of genius. Yes, that's how it felt as the 48 hours rolled over to 72, then on to 96. As the days turned into a week, finally the phone call came.

'Mr Webster? It's Norton Finance here.'

'Yes, yes!' I replied eagerly. Shouldn't that be Father Christmas or better still Jesus Christ my saviour?

My mind then went into a blur as the not so cheery Miss Stern rattled off their calculations for and against my loan request. They had come to the conclusion that, combined with my credit rating and even taking into consideration that I was a homeowner, the best that they could offer me as a loan was … £3,000. Now, if I would like to proceed they would send all the paperwork on to me and the money would be available in about four to six weeks. What do those adverts on the TV say again? Borrow up to £100,000? Instant access? Peace of mind? Well, peace of mind, my arse! My brain soon got into gear when she asked again if I would be proceeding with the loan. I seem to remember offloading some diatribe about how ridiculous an offer it was and how long I'd waited for them to get back to me and what a bunch of bullshitting liars they all were. But of course by this time she was long gone. I came to learn that at the slightest hint of a raised voice the call is terminated. I don't know what they quite expect from their clientele who are generally made up of stressed out, struggling and financially troubled people. Surely we should be allowed to get a bit hot under the collar sometimes? But no, because ultimately they are there to profit *from* your misery, not as it says on their adverts to help you *out* of your misery. Even if I had accepted their paltry sum, by the time they had got it all back by monthly repayments it worked out at about £7,000.

As I say, Norton was the first of many I contacted and,

over the time, I began to enjoy the calls with my request for more outlandish amounts for my loan. I even got up to £125,000 once just for the hell of it and I also perfected my technique of whispering down the phone in a very articulate manner that they were still a bunch of bullshitting liars and how ridiculous their offer was. I still didn't get the loan but at least they couldn't put the phone down on me for shouting! So, another avenue had been closed down and the debts of mortgage repayments and general living were ever mounting and that's without the VAT and income tax and the interest on that amount. Like any troubles you do get periods of respite or a 'ceasefire' as I like to refer to it. Maybe a week goes by or even ten days if you're lucky when a phone call doesn't come or a letter of demand doesn't arrive on your doormat. At these times one would think the stress would diminish and enjoyment of one's life would return. It does, but it's always tempered by that nagging feeling that something is coming… and it ain't going to be nice!

LET'S HOPE THIS PROPERTY CRASHES
ON A LOAN SHARK

Webbo's Guide to 'When All Around You Are Losing Their Heads, You Obviously Haven't Got a Grasp of the Situation.'

Learn how to whisper

Make sure you are prepared for a long and strained wait to hear the outcome of your loan application. Try to keep a cool head and learn the art of making your point through a whisper.

It's a great idea… for someone else to invest in

Never close yourself off to ways of trying to raise money to relieve your problem. But never make the mistake of plunging your ever-shrinking cash flow into it, however good it seems. Leave that to people who can afford it. Great ideas need a good venture capitalist. It's difficult to remain a company director when you're bankrupt.

Don't spend it until you've been lent it

Try not to get too excited about promises of money from financial institutions until you have the cash in your hand. Don't fantasise about it and certainly don't spend it on the notion that it's definitely coming. When the cheque has cleared, for however much it is, only then can you enjoy it.

Financial recovery guru Ian Cadlock says

Most insolvency practitioners would have advised Gary against both his property venture and applying for new loans. Opting for an IVA (Individual Voluntary Arrangement) at this stage would have been a realistic alternative. An IVA is essentially a contract between the debtor and his or her creditors, arranging for as much as can reasonably be expected from any surplus income to be paid back for a defined duration, at the end of which the creditor writes off any remaining shortfall. An IVA is less rigid than bankruptcy, and can have more beneficial terms, eg. lower costs than bankruptcy and more effective realisation of whatever assets may be offered.

'Let the good times roll!'

Gary and Phil take their roles as judges of the Hawaiian Tropic beach babes seriously.

Gary, left, on his wedding day, with best man Phil Middlemiss.

The happy couple: Gary and Wendy on their wedding day.

The cast of *Family Affairs*.

The Bill does *Little Britain*: Gary as the only gay in the village, with Bernie Nolan.

Gary with *Family Affairs* co-star Richard Hawley.

A winning storyline. Gary with members of the *Family Affairs* cast at the British Soap Awards. (Thanks to Paul Smith, IPC Media)

6

Buddy, Can You Spare A Dime?

In this country we have seen a rapid increase in debt over the last five years undoubtedly fuelled by a greater increase in the availability to borrow the damned stuff in the first place. The problems of the borrow-now-and-pay-later philosophy have always been highlighted but the golden rules are all too easy to ignore. *Don't borrow more than you can afford to pay back.* Forget that! How many times a day are we bombarded with images of things we *need* – that new car, that romantic holiday, that new coat, that new flat screen TV? All around us we see affluence and a society that spends, spends, spends. If we have to borrow in order to keep up, then so be it and to hell with the consequences. And this is where a curious British problem rears its head. I believe that as a nation, once trouble begins, we feel almost bound to deal with it ourselves – us and us alone. So when the trouble begins to escalate so does our need to keep it a secret from everyone else. 'It's my problem: I got myself into it and it's down to me to get myself out of it.' Now that is all very worthy but in the end that attitude will affect your health and just exacerbate the problem.

Fortunately I've always been able to sleep at night and things that have happened during the day are not likely to keep me awake during the wee small hours. I know I am very lucky in that respect because, for many, the endless nights of tossing and turning can be hell. Usually these financial problems prey on your mind because they are yours and yours alone or rather you allow them to be only yours. It is far better to talk to your partner or a family loved one at the end of a bad day than just to yourself. Battling against the world is tough when you try and do it on your own. Talking and sharing, I guarantee, will make it easier. No war was ever won by an individual working alone. It takes an army to do that so at my lowest point I got my army together. Wendy and I, friends and family, took each battle as it came together. It does work.

I can think of no worse situation than a man or woman with a mountain of debts and no foreseeable way to pay or even reduce them, waiting for the children and then their partner to go to bed to leave them in the darkness weeping at what to do next, contemplating all options of life as well as death. A dramatic scenario you might think but statistics prove that this scene is far from uncommon and more often than not it's the norm. As tough as it might be, my advice is that to overcome the problem you must confront the problem, and almost like a recovering addict *admit* to it – not just to yourself but to others too. Once this has been done, the weight of shame and helplessness begins to lift and advice can be sought on how to tackle the misery of your lack of funds. As an actor, I have always had the good fortune to enjoy the process of communication … it's what we actors do. Whether it be a character on stage or screen or down the pub on a proper night out we have a licence to talk about all things from football to not getting a part, to the death of someone close. We must be able to tap into a full range of emotions or how else would we be able to portray them to a wider audience? So it has never really been a great problem for me when asked to convey the seriousness of my financial situation and at certain times ask for help.

I believe this attitude is one that has kept me sane during the troubled periods and I would advise all others to try and do the same. I guess everyone needs their family and friends around to understand and help alleviate the problem. That does not have to be monetary of course: a simple listening ear over a coffee can mean as much as a cheque in the post. To have both is rare and extremely precious. My mum and immediate family, as in my brother Nick, have always been there when I've had to ask for help, but I guess, especially with family, I always like to make any loan conditional to make sure the repayment is as swift and regular as possible. To have a mate where even those restrictions are vetoed is to be very fortunate indeed. In Philip Middlemiss I have such a mate.

The history of me, Middo and money has been long and started when we were both sharing a flat in the late 80s (a two-bedroom flat I hasten to add before we are both offered lifetime membership at Foo Foo Lemar's in Manchester) and were just starting out on our roller-coaster ride to 'international stardom'. Back then, when I had just landed a part in *EastEnders* for three months and Middo had just finished a theatre run we set about thinking up ways to make some extra cash. These think tank sessions usually took place down at the Penge Snooker Club where, after a few frames, we would ensconce ourselves at the £150 jackpot slot machine and idly spend the rest of the afternoon trying to land the 'big one'. Both of us even gave our agents the snooker club's telephone number so we could be contacted there for any job interviews. On the rare occasions that the jackpot came up, regardless of whoever had financed the gamble out of his dole cheque, all winnings would be shared 50-50. That's how it was, how it is and how it will always be.

It was around this time, after one of our longer and more lubricated sessions at the Penge Snooker Club, that we created Starlight Management – Public Appearance Agents to the Stars. It is with great fondness that I remember going back to my hometown of Brentwood and standing in an almost empty wine bar whilst Middo (now under the name of Tony Pearce, Starlight's Managing Director) demanded our money in cash and argued that it wasn't his fault that nobody in the town appeared to be a fan of *EastEnders*. After a compromise of half the money in cash and half in 'all we could drink' we were satisfied with £100 each in our pocket. Thus our empire had begun! That was to be my first and only appearance for Starlight, but not for Middo, as it soon came to pass that the great Middo shalt play the bookmaker Des Barnes in the great *Coronation Street*. In 1991, Starlight Management re-formed under the new ownership of Trevor Pearce (that's right, Tony's brother, and yes, right again, yours truly, now 18 months unemployed). Sitting opposite Middo in our flat negotiating (as Trevor) with the marketing manager of Ladbrokes for Des Barnes to open their new non-smoking shop in Llandudno was probably my finest performance ever. Certainly having to stifle Middo's fits of laughter while negotiating the expenses was not easy. And so it happened that Des Barnes did open the shop although the marketing manager advised Middo to think about dropping his agent Trevor Pearce and next time go directly to her. What a harsh and fickle world showbiz was, and still is. The lady in question still does not know that I was in fact Trevor Pearce but I'm sure the owner of the wine bar in Brentwood has often told people how the bloke who plays Des Barnes in *Coronation Street* used to be a dodgy agent who called himself Tony Pearce!

Every so often when having to clear out old files and things from the loft I come across the business cards we had printed up for Starlight Management and they never fail to raise a smile for a simpler time. But any money lent or borrowed has always been unconditional. It's tough enough to ask for a little help with the mortgage or for the Christmas period but to feel that you will have conditions attached to that loan is really hard. It is something that I've never experienced with Middo. When all roads were closing down to me and letters and demands were hitting the door mat at the rate of Pete Doherty's drug convictions, Middo was there to help out. And how did he do it? He asked what kind of sum would be a help and I told him as honestly as I could how much would give us a few months breathing space. He told me that a cheque would be in the post, which it was.

Now this was a cheque for a five figure sum and was crucial to our financial survival at that time, especially over Christmas 2004 to 2005. The cover note that accompanied the cheque said *'Put it all on black!'* – a reference to the roulette table that Philip and I had often frequented in casinos. That was his only judgment, his only comment, and it was a fantastic gesture from a true friend. It was all the more poignant because it was a reminder of one of the greatest of all nights when we had indeed *put it all on black* to break the bank at Monte Carlo (or at least a win at the Gloucester Road Casino). Our friends Sam and Fidel had informed us that they and a few mates were going to Amsterdam for the weekend and it would be great if Middo and I could make up the numbers. The only problem was the cost. Neither having worked for a few months, we had no spare cash. It was simple: we needed £200 each or we could not go to Amsterdam. It was time to *speculate to accumulate*.

Taking £50 each out of our very beleaguered bank accounts, Middo and I set off, appropriately suited and booted, to the Gloucester Road Casino an establishment that had served us well during our three fun packed years of drama school. Our aim was to go black and low on the roulette table and thus raise the needed booty for the weekend in Amsterdam. After several hours of grinding out a little extra money at the blackjack table I moved alongside Middo at the roulette table. He was doing well, about £75 up, and together with my £30 profit we had a pot of about £200 to play with. We bet first 18, second 18, third 18, odds and evens, black and red, slowly building, slowly building. The tension was only pierced when free drinks and canapés were served to the longstanding members of the table. Middo slung me a look of horror when his James Bond persona was shattered as I announced in a voice that would hit the back wall of The

National Theatre, 'Hey, Middo – grub up!' and offered him a turkey roll sandwich.

The tension continued to increase until, upon looking down we both realised that we had £500 on the table! We'd done it – we were going to Amsterdam! For me, the time had come to cash in … or so I thought. Middo coolly eyed the chips, stacked them together and pushed them back onto the shimmering green baize and quietly whispered, '*Put it all on black*.' He turned to smile at my now blubbering face as the ball was dropped on to the spinning wheel. I couldn't look. He didn't have to – he instinctively knew what was going to happen. 'Ten black' was the cry from the croupier. *Now* was the time to cash in. A word was not spoken by the two of us until we had left the casino, feigning dejected loss past the two doormen so as not to waste any money tipping them. Once outside, an extremely large high five took place and a scream of utter delight was let out that could be heard in Crystal Palace where Sam and Fidel were waiting for news of our efforts. So when Middo's cheque arrived with the recommendation to *put it all on black* (though of course I didn't), I know that Philip would have been equally proud if I secretly had.

"PUT IT ALL ON BLACK"

Webbo's Guide to Begging With Style

Happy, happy, happy... happy talk

Always communicate to others how you are feeling and the effect your troubles are having on you. Great if it's your partner or friend, or even go to your doctor. If you slip into depression life will take on an even tougher slant. Prescription drugs for depression and an unrelated person's knowledge of your situation can be a great help.

Des Barnes and all that

If you can, have the faith to trust a true friend who will support you through any circumstances. Remember, there should be no shame and no blame.

The name's Bond... James Bond

In the language of sensible casino etiquette, where matters of finance are concerned always have a plan of attack, know what your limits are, and remember that there is no shame in quitting while you are ahead.

7

The Net Closes In

We survived Christmas 2004 without any major hiccups: We put Middo's money towards the good causes of the two mortgages, made a small gesture-of-goodwill payment to the VAT and of course ensured Father Christmas had enough cash to pay the elves to make the children's Christmas presents. I set about the New Year with a renewed vigour, trying to raise the money to pay off all the VAT and income-tax payments and keep the wolves from our terraced door. But it didn't take long before things began to get on top again. I still couldn't match my outgoings to my income and of course it's always around Christmas and post Christmas when all the payments have to go out and yet there's nothing extra coming in. Suddenly by March I was getting hit with two mortgage payments, a council tax payment (in full as the previous year's had gone into arrears) and a ground rent demand for the flat that sent a shiver down my spine. By the time the water, the gas, the electric, BT and T-Mobile came on board I was going into overload. I fully identify with that feeling that many people I have spoken to describe as a trance-like state. You are being hit from all sides, but you seem to become oblivious to it all, hoping that it will go away of its own accord and that you will suddenly awake from your grey hypnotic state and be in the sunshine. But unless your six numbers come up that ain't going to happen. I simply had to try and take a grip of this ever slippery bar of financial soap.

I had to push as hard as I could for a loan on the flat. After speaking to my financial adviser and my accountant we set about raising more money via the mortgage company. In short we wanted to remortgage, a common, almost effortless occurrence for many, but not for me. Letting your mortgage repayments go into arrears on a couple of occasions does not boost the confidence of your financial lender. But given the choice between feeding your kids, or letting the mortgage slide for a month, well there really is no decision to make. So Bill set about persuading the mortgage company that I was worth the risk. I knew I was but would they? A £50,000 remortgage would really buy me some time. I could make real inroads into paying off some debts and it would give me that freedom to wait until the housing market had picked up again so the flat could be sold for a decent amount. Hell, it could be rented out in the meantime, covering the cost of one of those crippling mortgage payments. As long as I was still working everyone would eventually be paid off. We had a plan and we could at last look forward. Who was I kidding? You know what I said earlier about a trance-like state? Well, that is a fine example of one. By taking out loans to pay off loans the problem just gets bigger and deeper.

I remember looking at my work schedule with glee when I realised that I had a morning off – an ideal opportunity to arrange a meeting with a loan company who, via the Internet, had hinted that I could borrow the sum of £30,000. Bill was still working on the mortgage company to come up with the funds but I felt compelled to put some hard work in too. So I rushed around to their offices in Brentford to plead for my money (Wendy, Jack and Freddie came too in order to reinforce the notion of a family in need). I put on my best furrowed brow and most convincing here's-a-man-who-is-trustworthy-of-course-we'll-lend-him-thirty-thousand-pounds look. But alas, like every route I had taken before, it was closed down to me. My credit rating was now too low. An arrears had showed up on my mortgage payments, I was overdrawn too regularly at the bank, and everything that they had promised would not be a problem in their ads most certainly was now.

I guess that it was beginning to dawn on me that I might not be able to get out of this situation, and I began to fear the worst. This was compounded by one particular incident that happened at our home while I was stuck in the studio filming. I need just say two words to get any self-respecting debt-ridden person's hackles to rise… the bailiff. At the end of this section there will be a few pointers on how to deal with the dreaded bailiff that may hold you in good stead if one should ever come knocking at your door. I am sure the Union of Debt Collectors, to give them their joined-up-writing title, would say that ours was an isolated incident but I feel that the nation probably knows that that may be stretching the term 'isolated' a little too far. Having returned to my dressing-room after a particularly intensive morning of about ten scenes, I picked up my messages. My blood began to boil as Wendy's message told me how she was in the kitchen with a crying Freddie, a confused Jack and an unwanted guest in the shape of a bailiff who was demanding about £1,300 in unpaid council tax. Should this not materialise he was sizing up what he was going to take in lieu of the money.

I put the phone down before the message finished and rang Wendy immediately. She answered tearfully and I could hear Freddie in the background. I have never felt more angry and helpless. I asked her to put the man on the phone. After a long and heated argument in which he held all the trump cards, we eventually agreed that he would give me half an hour to ring through a payment on my debit card to pay the arrears. As soon as his company confirmed this payment he would leave. Never have I been more desperate for my card not to let me down. It didn't. I rang Wendy straightaway and told her to tell him to get out of our house. I would have told him myself but such was the intensity of the heat generated by our last conversation that he now refused to speak to me.

Wendy asked him to leave but he refused as he had not yet had confirmation from his office that the payment had been made. Fifteen minutes later Wendy rang me to say the office had just called and he was now gone. She then burst into tears again, or rather howled like an animal in pain. Her utter misery was made worse by the bailiff's departing comments that he had been clocking everything in the house such as the computer, the television, etc. because he assumed that one day he would be coming back. At that very point if he had been in my company I would have willingly done three months at Belmarsh Prison just for the satisfaction of battering the smug bastard into the next street. But I couldn't because I wasn't there, a regret I will have for the rest of my life. This was made tougher for me by learning what had happened after he had left...

Jack had asked his mummy why she was upset. Wendy, obviously not wanting to distress the children (our policy throughout), told Jack she was tearful because we were a bit short of money at the present time but there was nothing to worry about. Five minutes later Jack came into the kitchen where Wendy was now sitting with a much needed black coffee. He handed Wendy his treasured money box and told her she could have all the money he had saved up. It was the richest £3.85 Wendy had ever been offered. Wendy burst into tears again and gave Jack the biggest hug ever.

That one incident, more than any other, made me realise that whatever happened from now on I must always keep on top of my finances and must be clued up on all law regarding can and can't dos regarding debt recovery. I also resolved to write this book – to put all this down on paper in order to help other people going through a similar situation and to highlight and expose the sometimes despicable practices of these bullies and thugs who pose as debt recovery agency officials. And don't forget the mob who came to see us were employed by the local county council! I was always led to believe that the council is supposed to serve the community and to care about the society which pays its wages, not to use a sarcastic threatening enforcement agency to scare and upset depressed people as it goes about its dirty work.

All of this was gradually leading to the point where no amount of juggling money and no amount of making phone calls putting off payments would matter any more. Basically the net was closing in and pretty soon the only word that could be filed under my name would be 'bankrupt'. But that time was not quite yet. Over the past few months leading up to June 2005 my accountant had been in conversation with the VAT and Inland Revenue offices pleading my case constantly and explaining that I was doing everything possible to raise the cash to repay the debt. To their credit the guys and gals from the City Hall's best had given me more than enough leeway to do just that. But there comes a time when they will wait no longer and I knew that by the month of May that time had come. But first there were things to enjoy – work, work and work! At the beginning of May, as is customary in the TV calendar, the British Soap Awards reared its beautiful head again and three weeks beforehand we all waited with bated breath for the nominations to come out.

Webbo's Expert Guide to Dealing With Stress

It's true what they say after Christmas

I know we've all heard it a million times before, but do realise that you will be hit hard in January and February regarding bills and repayments. Try to keep your festive season spending under control and do not use it as an excuse to have a blow out to forget about your troubles. Believe me, they will come back at you twice as nasty.

You can't cancel the council

There are certain outgoings that, once you have got past the point of negotiation with the claimant, become very hard to avoid. Be aware that the caring welfare state has vanished. If your phone bill is a few weeks overdue they will cut you off. It's the same with water, gas and electricity. The council will employ harsh tactics too to get their money. If you know you are going to struggle, get a repayment scheme firmly in place regardless of how little or how much you are paying every month. Try also to make it a direct debit – it's one less thing to worry about.

Bastards

Once the bailiff is involved, things can get very scary and very nasty. Make sure you read up on your legal rights regarding debt recovery and with that knowledge don't be afraid to act on it. Know your rights – people fought and died for them. Be assured, if they can bend and abuse your said rights, the bailiffs will, Statistics tell us there's more bad 'uns than good 'uns.

Financial recovery guru Ian Cadlock says

Consult an expert. An insolvency practitioner has the expert knowledge that your everyday accountant may not be aware of, and his/her aim is to find positive outcomes for debtors, creditors and anyone else involved in this kind of situation.

8

A Night Of Triumph

'And the winner is... Marlon from *Emmerdale*! The British Soap Award for Best Dramatic Performance 2004 goes to actor Mark Charnock.'!

Ah, the hurt and the pain of defeat. Twelve months earlier in 2004 my great friend and fellow actor Kazia Pelka had given one of the performances of her life as Chrissie Costello in *Family Affairs*. Over six months, the nation (or 1.2 million viewers at least) had watched transfixed as Chrissie (my wife in the show) had fooled me, our family and all the good folk of the fictitious London Borough of Charnham that our nine-year-old daughter had cancer. In actual fact the character of Chrissie was suffering from Munchausen Syndrome and was heading straight for a nervous breakdown. Kazia's superb potrayal of a woman on the edge had gained plaudits from everyone, and after being nominated for her dramatic performance, everyone at *Family Affairs* thought that maybe, for the first time in its eight years, it might actually win something. My comments from the after show party that night were, 'She was robbed!' Kazia lost out to a good performance from the very gracious Mark Charnock. So when the nominations for 2005 revealed that not only had Kazia been nominated for her performance but also the Costello family as a whole (for

'Best Storyline'), we were very excited… but we were not holding our breath.

In fact a right good Duffetting was the order of the day when producers and executives and most of the cast met at the Hilton Hotel in Kensington before moving *en masse* to BBC TV Centre to enjoy the night's proceedings. The Soap Awards have built up a reputation for being a really good night out that goes long into the small hours, usually of the next morning and the morning after. As I said earlier in this recollection, working on a soap is about as intense as it can get in the entertainment profession. The awards night allows everyone from the production to cast and crew to let their hair down and just enjoy and celebrate the good work that British soaps do. Having said that, there are still the basics to adhere to – interviews, posing for pictures, sitting nicely for three hours, clapping, laughing and cheering in all the right places and going mad at the party after going away empty handed for the umpteenth time.

Even though I've been acting for some twenty years now one never stops learning, certainly one's craft but all the peripheral bits as well. I remember with great affection the way Kazia taught me how to make an entrance. Before entering the venue of the British Soap Awards there's a small section of red carpet with reporters and photographers lined up on each side. Such is the fickle business of being a celebrity that you are only in demand until someone more famous comes along behind you, at which point you are waved aside like a troublesome fly before the circus moves on. I love the work side of the profession but have never taken seriously the other aspects – my ego just isn't large enough. Hence my natural instinct is to bypass the queue for the carpet and get straight to the bar. Sensing this, Kazia decided to teach the master a few tricks.

'Wait,' she whispered, 'wait, wait…' We held hands and under Kazia's firm grip we waited until the red carpet ahead of us was empty, probably for the first time that night. Behind us the guests were still backing up but by now all the *EastEnders* and *Coronation Street*, stars were in the building. *'Now,'* was the demand from Kazia and we began to walk. We were hit with a barrage of flashlights and reporters shouting for our attention. Eventually we arrived in the reception hall. I turned to my co-star, kissed her on the hand, and said, 'Now *that's* how you walk the red carpet!' My education was complete.

Once settled into our seats we set about keeping ourselves amused for the next three hours. The host, Paul O'Grady, was at his usual caustic best and indeed the highlights of the show, for much of the audience, were his quips during the ad breaks when recording stops. There is no finer wit in Britain than Paul and when on form, he is truly a pleasure to watch. Eventually we got round to the Panel Awards – the Soap Awards which are not voted for by the public but by an esteemed group made up of TV and newspaper critics and TV pundits. These were the awards to win as it was down to a discerning eye rather than a straightforward popularity vote, which always sees the likes of *EastEnders*, *Coronation Street* and *Emmerdale* winning. In short, the critics' vote allowed soaps such as

Hollyoaks and *Family Affairs* to be in with a chance. But as I've said before, this was a very slim chance as previous barren years had shown us.

'And now on to Best Dramatic Performance,' Paul O'Grady told the now packed audience. The nominations were read out and, oblivious to all other names, we all waited for 'Kazia Pelka'. As it was read out we all clapped and cheered and I turned to Kazia and wished her good luck. She deserved to win it and something happened that gave me the idea she would be going home with the prize this year. In all the time I have known Kazia (and that dates back to our days at drama school), no one has *ever* pronounced her name right the first time. It is always Cassie or Kedja or even Cissie. But never Kazia.

The celebrity who read out the nominations pronounced her name perfectly, which suggested to me she had been practising. But why? Could it possibly be? No, we dared not dream but we were about to find out as the envelope was opened. And the winner is (perfectly pronounced) Kazia Pelka . Time seemed to stand still as Kazia turned to me. It was a great moment. I congratulated her and was genuinely pleased as Kazia and *Family Affairs* had finally got the respect they deserved. The *Family Affairs* section of the audience – the producers, writers, directors, cast and crew erupted. Eight years of hurt had never stopped us dreaming. *It's coming home, it's coming home, acting's coming home!* Whatever happened now with the Best Storyline award, win or lose, *Family Affairs* could rightly call itself 'an award-winning soap'. But like a London bus, when you wait forever for one it doesn't come, then two or three come along at once. So it was with the Soap Awards 2005. Would you believe it? We won Best Storyline as well!

By this time anyone connected with *Family Affairs* was in Pinot Grigio dreamland. Kazia, Leah Coombs, Harry Capehorn and I went up to accept the award and it was left to me to say a few words. Realising that this was certainly the first and possibly my last opportunity to accept an award, I took on the mantle to deliver our acceptance speech. After praising the producers past and present and everybody else I thought of who could give me future employment (it's called arse licking), and highlighting how good Kazia had been and so on... there was only one thing left to say. I regaled the Nicola Duffett story and announced to the audience and the viewing millions that we were off to get 'Duffetted'! Those who knew Nicola were texting her before the night was through to reveal that going on a night out with her was now famous. Nicola has been extremely grateful ever since.

As I looked through bleary eyes the next morning at my Soap Award I happily mulled over the final score – *EastEnders* 8; *Coronation Street* 6; *Family Affairs* 2; *Emmerdale*, *Hollyoaks* and *Doctors* 1 each – not bad for an under-advertised, under-supported (by Channel 5) show that went out at 6.30 in the evening. Little did we know that on *Family Affairs'* night of triumph the powers that be at Channel 5 had already planned its demise. Nothing ever surprises me in my chosen profession, and the only answer I have ever given to *Family Affairs* being pulled off the air is that, 'Of course, when the show is getting its best ratings ever, has assembled its best cast ever, and has just won two prestigious British Soap Awards, *of course* that's when you axe it!' Channel 5 may have had its own strange reasoning and one has to just go with the flow but to replace *Family Affairs* with the non award-winning ratings disaster *Joey*? Come on! But the public knows what *Family Affairs* was and what it represented – the public always does. But on that hung-over Sunday morning, the sun was glinting off my new shiny Soap Award, my wife and children were healthy, and for a short moment all was well with the Webster world.

The next morning I opened what I had been dreading – a brown envelope with the Royal Courts of Justice stamp on it. A court time and date had been set for a petition of bankruptcy against a certain Gary Ian Webster. Me! I now look back at my constitution and my somewhat crazy (possibly warped) humour with great pride. Without really batting an eyelid I folded up the petition and placed it behind my Soap Award, which was now standing tall in the kitchen cabinet. I couldn't have dreamed of a better analogy for an image of the agony and the ecstasy than that, and I couldn't help but burst into fits of laughter. Sometimes you just have to go with the flow and smile at the cards that life has dealt you.

Webbo's Expert Guide to Winning

Dry clean your suit

Don't do as I did and get hammered the night before an awards ceremony, only to wake up mid-morning and find your one and only suit needs cleaning. For a good night out, much like financial management, keep everything in good order.

Where did I put my speech?

Allow your natural optimism to reign and always prepare for winning by having your acceptance speech ready. On being asked whether mine was made up on the spot, I had to admit I'd been practising it for weeks, just in case. As for award ceremonies, as for finance – prepare, prepare, prepare.

Three cheers for Gareth

As in any line of work, always make sure you are sharing your space with a top person. *Family Affairs* was a team effort, but in the confines of our dressing-room I could not have asked for a better cell mate than Gareth Hale. He was always there for support during my troubled year.

9
One More Try

So there it was in black and white – 21 June 2005 at 11 a.m. – my date with destiny. I rang Bill and asked for the law on the situation. It was really quite simple – if I could come up with the required £35,000, the petition would be withdrawn and I was off the hook. If not I would go bust, tits up, up the Swanee without a paddle... that's right, bankrupt! However, all was not lost. Bill informed me that Tony Gough (my financial adviser who had come on board at Bill's invitation to try and get me out of my predicament) was trying very hard to get my mortgage company to understand and give me a loan on my mortgage. I cannot thank Bill and Tony enough for trying so hard to keep the wolves from my door. In the end, if Bill says to me, 'Make sure you put some money aside for tax,' and I don't do it, then there is no one else to blame but Gary Webster. Bill was always understanding and always trying to make the best of my bad situation. Believe me, when all the dark clouds are gathering and you need to hear a comforting, reassuring voice, there is no better person to ring than Bill Shaw.

So, my last drink at the last chance saloon was to raise the money needed from the remortgage of my flat. There was nothing more I could do really but work, be happy and positive and wait to hear the mortgage company's decision. In troubled times I think that if you look hard enough you can always find a ray of light and hope out of the smallest gap in the dark. Ours came courtesy of Ron Howard. That's right, Richie Cunningham from *Happy Days,* Fonz's best friend turned director of such blockbuster movies as *Cocoon, Apollo 13*, etc. How on earth, I hear you asking, could Ron Howard be my ray of light? Let me explain…

When you are short of money, in need of money, or just desperate for money you find yourself looking at ways to make the said green stuff all over the place – schemes, ideas, investments, even competitions. You find yourself ringing up all available quiz show question lines to try and win £1,000 here or a new car there, and so it was with us. Being film and trivia nuts, our natural leaning was toward celebrities and the entertainment industry. We found ourselves (Wendy and I that is, not me and Ron Howard!) on the Internet trying to identify the personality from a photograph showing only his or her eyes – a competition seen numerous times in weekly soap magazines. The game is, if you think you know the personality, just from his or her eyes, you text your answer to the number given. If correct, you are guaranteed the winning sum of money *in cash*, within 24 hours.

And so it came to pass that on this particular day, for the princely sum of £5,000, I could see that those were the eyes of the great Ron. Immediately we texted through RON HOWARD. Almost as immediately it came back that we were CORRECT and had won the £5,000 in cash! We were then instructed to text back our address so an operative from the telecommunications quiz company could come and deliver the cash personally. We could not believe it. This was our first piece of monetary luck in a year! As it stood, every cent of our money, borrowed or earned, was going out to pay off our loans, our mortgages and our ever mounting debts. This was the first lump sum we could use for some of the pleasures in life – a family holiday, perhaps, and certainly for some goodies over the Christmas period. Like any parents we didn't want the children to suffer over Christmas. Wendy was ecstatic and all that night I knew she was tossing and turning, thinking about what we could spend this bonus cash on. After I convinced her that this money mustn't be spent on booking a table for four at The Ivy, we agreed that it would most certainly be spent on the children and maybe a gesture of some sort to all those who were helping us out.

Now, what I've been writing about all through this journey of mine is that when you think you've got it sussed you almost certainly haven't. In short, when you are in the shit you only seem to go in deeper. Twenty-four hours came and went... as did forty-eight... as did three and four and five days. The money seemed to be unobtainable, as indeed was the telephone number of the competition company. Fate was not to be so cruel with us was it? It was. Our pants had been well and truly taken down. This was when Wendy came into her own – she was not going to take this lying down; we'd won that five grand fair and square! Those were Ron Howard's eyes damn it, and that cash was ours! Wendy quickly put through a call to Mark Stephens, a personal friend who just happens to be one of the best media lawyers in London. Mark pointed us in exactly the right direction and after several phone calls and letters to OFTEL (the telecommunications regulator) and CICSTIS we eventually, several months later, received a cheque for £5,000. By this time a cheque was the last thing we needed as it got swallowed up into my great black hole of bankruptcy. At this point I realised what Wendy was going on about when she had said, 'It's not the principle it's the money!'

So, while this six degrees of separation was happening between myself and Ron Howard, 21 June 2005 was looming ever closer. A meeting was arranged for me to meet up with Bill and Tony to see if a final decision had been made on the loan. If the decision was in our favour we would then have to work as hard as we could to get the released money to the courts and subsequently to the VAT office before 21 June. The omens were good: GMAC had approved the loan and the forms were all signed... that was the good news. The bad news was that it would take five working days for the money to come through. I had just three days, taking into account the weekend. Bill promised to get all the paperwork concerning the loan to the lawyers at the VAT office to confirm that the money was coming, but he did explain that it might be a day or two short of the deadline.

We agreed on this strategy and then we all looked for a large slice of luck. The following week 21 June came and went. I heard nothing – no notification and no ominous looking letter from the Royal Courts of Justice. I now began to believe that our promise of money had been

82

accepted and that the nightmare was over. After several days of checking with the *Family Affairs* publicity department that no journalist had been wanting to speak to me on a 'personal matter', I was confident enough to really look forward to the coming weekend. We decided that Wendy should spend it with the children at her parents'. This would allow Wendy to relax, the children to have lots of fun in the country, and me to go out and have a beer in celebration of the fact that we had stopped the rot.

So after having a relaxed and lubricated Friday night, I awoke on the Saturday to find the usual array of junk mail on the doormat, underneath of which I also saw the brown corner of a somewhat larger envelope. My own words of wisdom ran through my head: *'Never open your mail on a Saturday because whatever it is can't be dealt with until Monday anyway.'* But I had to open this. I sat on the stairs and carefully unpicked the gum off the flap. I hoped upon hope that I would find a Willy Wonka golden ticket, but alas it was not to be. The letter was indeed from the Royal Courts of Justice and the hardest pill now had to be swallowed. I had been declared bankrupt on 21 June 2005 at 11 a.m – the longest day. The letter informed me that I was to meet with the Official Receiver in three weeks' time; I had to bring with me all my relevant financial details and must be prepared to stay all day.

A strange dichotomy of sadness and relief came over me – it was now out of my hands and, in a strange way, life might now get some structure to it. There were rules that had to be adhered to by law and all the demands from creditors would now stop. The phone calls would cease and a knock at the door was not to be feared. I remember calling Wendy to let her know the bad but not disastrous news. I reassured her that all was not lost as I still had my job and indeed I was in the process of negotiating a new and improved contract. Imagine the phone call I had to make the following Monday in which I told Wendy that the bit about the job wasn't exactly true. I explained that we had just heard that they were going to axe the show. Amazing, but that's exactly how it happened. Just for the record, I missed my remortgage money coming through to pay off the VAT debt by just three days. Red tape and paperwork – the bane of every budding bankrupt the world over.

So that was it – I was bankrupt, bust, but I didn't feel any different. A little more humble maybe, disappointed *definitely* – that I had allowed the situation to build over the years, especially when I finally got my act together with my wife and children. But I was still breathing, nobody had died... the word wasn't 'cancer', or 'terminal' or 'fatal', it was simply 'bankrupt'. A new, if somewhat different life, was about to begin but it was one to attack and make good from and that's what I had set out to do.

Webbo's Expert Guide To The End Is Nigh

Try, try and try again

Always keep going in the face of adversity. It may not eventually work out but you'll keep your self-esteem and it always looks good on the CV to the Official Receiver. It shows you were always willing to try.

The eyes are the windows of the soul

Never forget that every morning is a new day and things can change. For me, it came in the shape of Ron Howard. Hopefully next time it will be a female, but however you look at it, it was a good thing to happen. Remember, you have to be in it to win it.

There are no definites in life

Just what it says on the packet – always try to see the worst case scenario along with the best. Things can and do get worse before they get better, but being prepared for that keeps you on the front foot and in control. There's no gain without pain.

Financial recovery guru Ian Cadlock says

Putting off bankruptcy is not necessarily a good idea. Bankruptcy by this stage was inevitable, and Gary would have saved himself a huge amount of stress over a long period if he had taken this option earlier. The reality of bankruptcy was nowhere near as much of a monster as Gary had assumed.

10

The End Is Just The Beginning

As I've said, my main constant and saviour through all of my troubled financial times was that I was still working on *Family Affairs*. Although sometimes difficult, it was a wonderful distraction in the best sense of the word. It allowed me to focus on other things apart from the financial disaster happening around me. I certainly feel, as an actor, I did some of my best work to date on that show. Although the announcement of its demise was a shock, it wasn't anything I couldn't handle compared to my roller-coaster year. Nicola Duffett and I took it upon us, as senior members of the cast, to rally the troops. Some of the younger cast members who had recently come into the show and were looking forward to a long run in an award-winning show may have been distressed by the news.

Who was it who said, 'The only thing certain in life is taxes, death and a long-running soap?' Well, liar, liar, pants on fire! We headed straight down the pub and then on to Nicola's to get Duffetted for one last time, all the while emphasising that we must *not* get bitter. My rallying cry was, 'I don't want to see anyone coming into work from now until the end with a *what's the point* attitude. That will not happen!' I slurred that until there were just a few of us hardened drinkers left.

To our horror we realised that the sun was now rising and it was time to go into work. That great line from *Singing in the Rain* came to mind – *Good morning, good morning, we've talked the whole night through, good morning, good morning to you*! Unfortunately we'd also drunk the whole night through and after some black coffee and a quick shower (not together, I hasten to add), Duffers and I headed into the *Family Affairs* studio, tired, emotional and very hung-over. I still remember the look on the faces of some of the young cast as one of the make-up artists noted that I needed a little extra help that morning. I retorted, 'Oh what's the point? Who cares? I'll go on like I am! We'll all be gone in five weeks anyway!' What a plonker I was – from Churchill to bitter pill in just one Duffetting. What an example! Fortunately everyone just burst out laughing and indeed we remained professional until the end.

As a financial wizard, however, my end had already come. At the weekend, ten days after my letter of bankruptcy, there was a little article in the *News of the World* to inform the public that it had happened. Knowing that my mother was a traditional *Mail on Sunday* reader I didn't fear the worst and was still preparing to tell her in my own time. That was to be short lived. On Sunday evening I received the dreaded phone call. Picking it up, I noted that my trousers were not around my ankles, indicating that it wasn't going to be extremely *bad* news. 'Gary, is everything okay?' she asked.

'Yes, no problems,' I replied.

Then with the subtlety of a Muslim celebrating Passover she blurted out, 'You've gone bankrupt, haven't you?'

The silence that followed told me that on the other end of the line tears were falling and I felt very sad that my mum should be so upset at something I had done, something which was not altogether good but not exactly heinous either. I think it's a generational thing.

After a few minutes (or was it hours) of reassuring her that it was not life or death, she started to tune in to the Gazza Webbo philosophy of life and its hard knocks. Upon more digging I realised that the way in which she had learned of my bankruptcy hadn't exactly helped. She had been stopped in the street by a supposed friend who offered her condolences upon the tragedy that had befallen me. Her exact words were, 'Kath, oh my dear, I'm so, *so* sorry to hear about Gary… what a terrible shame.'

I think my mum was expecting to find me on death row in Sing Sing for the brutal murder of a Channel 5 executive! But as I say, it's a generational thing. Still, that episode gave me good warning of what might be coming at work. If my mum had heard about it then probably everyone else had too. If there's one thing I can't stand it's gossiping, backbiting and whispers in darkened corners. So I thought I would be better off if I brought my predicament out into the open – that way nobody would feel it was a stigma and nobody would feel the need to avert my gaze on set or in the queue for lunch.

But how could I do it? I couldn't just call a meeting and announce that due to my ineptitude regarding monetary matters I had gone bankrupt. No, that option sounded far too serious and not my style. I finally decided to go with a humorous approach and it was with great relief that I was met with laughs and smiles and eventually a round of applause when I walked out on to a packed set of cast and crew to do my first scene of the day with a huge bucket that I needed both hands to carry. Emblazoned on the side of the bucket were the words: Bankrupt! All donations gratefully accepted!' And as I rattled the bucket I also shouted, 'Wife and two children to support!' to the gathered masses. Some months later at the end of series party people were still coming up to me to congratulate me on my spirit and attitude. Their support and affection is something I'll never forget.

So there it is, or rather there it was. My year – my crazy up-and-down year from illness and near death experiences to extremely funny situations, all leading to me finally being declared bankrupt. I am a great fatalist and really do think that my bankruptcy was inevitable and maybe had to be that extreme for me to get a grip on my monetary acumen. I see it as a cathartic experience, not always pleasant and not always nice but never life-threatening. Throughout the whole year I have seen the gamut of humanity from wholehearted support and friendship to downright bastardy from those working on the supposed 'right' side of the law.

As with any experience, to make it worthwhile you have to take the positives from it and above all learn from it. I believe that I've done this. I will not go down the same road again and will adhere more to the line 'only when all else has been paid can I spend it' rather than 'only when I have spent it all else can be paid?' I hope that anyone reading this account of bankruptcy will take from it the positives I try to instil. Certainly for anyone going through the same situation it has been written for *you*. Remember, it is not life or death, there is help out there. Always try to talk about the extent of your troubles, as hard as that may be. You can reap a far bigger reward from that attitude than a monetary one. And remember, while we are all living and breathing and *compos mentis* we have the power to change our situation. If we can start to do that we have already won.

As I tuck my two beautiful children up in bed and gaze lovingly at my beautiful wife, I am safe in the knowledge that throughout it all my bankruptcy has been a positive experience. I won't let it be anything else, for as I contemplate this idyllic scene, I have just opened a letter to my wife from the Royal Courts of Justice to inform her that her bankruptcy petition has been set for a date in three months' time. Now what did I say about two peas in a pod?

Webbo's Expert Guide To The Finishing Line... Of Sorts...

Mum's the word

Always be ready for the varying scale of reactions to your financial predicament, good and bad. As long as you have it in perspective, it really doesn't matter what anyone else thinks. Always be honest to your loved ones – it's only money after all – and if one's life is to be judged purely on one's crap financial sense, then they can blow it out their ass! Always have the good fortune to have a mum, like mine, who is understanding, helpful and with enough of a sense of humour to put up with her wayward son.

What's all the fuss about?

Strangely, once the name 'bankruptcy' comes to be joined at the hip with your own, a huge weight seems to be lifted. It's not great, but it's not the end. It should be seen as a new financially ordered beginning.

Living

Keep everything in moderation, except laughter. Keep positive and enthusiastic about all things. And above all... keep breathing.

Financial recovery guru Ian Cadlock says

Bankruptcy is as much of a privilege as a pain: while your assets are now all taken as a contribution to paying off your creditors, bankruptcy allows you to pass over all your pressing debt problems to the Official Receiver. As Gary felt, it can come as a relief.

11

Straightforward Answers To All The Crucial Questions

by Ian Cadlock, Insolvency Advisor, Tenon Recovery

? **I owe shit loads of money on a mountain of credit cards – can't I just go bankrupt and wipe the slate clean?**

Of course you can but look before you leap and ask yourself first, for instance, what assets might I lose?

? **I'm struggling to make the repayments on my loans and credit card. Is there any way I can keep these people happy without defaulting on the payments completely?**

Yes – there are lots of debt advice charities and bodies like CABs who will very likely get you a deal with your creditors but the sort of deal they'd go for is really not much more than an indefinite stopgap – your liabilities will hang around like bad smells for many years.

? **I've just lost my job and can't afford the repayments on a loan I took out last year. The account has been transferred to a debt collecting agency but they are really pressuring me to make payments, which I can't afford. What can I do?**

There are lots of options but just about all of them depend on some basic points such as:-

- Deal with all your creditors at once – not one at a time.
- If you can't pay all don't pay any – at least until you've got a deal binding on them all.
- Keep talking – creditors hate to be ignored and if you do that you'll find it harder later to get them on your side.
- Make sure you have the most and best information on your financial situation – you're going to have to tell them the whole story some time.

? Can a bailiff break into my house?

Yes but only in very strictly defined circumstances – for example if the bailiffs are trying to recover certain types of taxes and if you use force to prevent them entering peaceably.

? What kind of goods can't the bailiff take from my property?

Any goods that aren't yours, though you have to prove that, which is often difficult if not impossible. Also anything that can't be sold such as documents, or any goods that are obviously worth vastly more than the debt the bailiff is trying to collect. Apart from things like that, the bailiffs can take pretty much whatever they want.

? **I rent a furnished flat – can the bailiffs take things that aren't actually mine?**

Well, actually, they can if they haven't been given solid evidence to show that they're not yours – whoever does own the goods must give the bailiff the evidence within five days of seizure, and if it stacks up, the bailiff has to hand back the goods.

? **What kind of things can't the Official Receiver's office get their hands on (wedding ring, tools of your trade etc.)?**

When you go into bankruptcy all your assets immediately vest in it with the following exemptions:

- All your personal and domestic belongings, excepting any items that might have a fairly high value (usually £500+), and you have to be given enough money to buy replacements for any essential items.
- Tools of the trade – sometimes this is obvious, but sometimes not. These days it's quite common for a low value car or a computer to be accepted as necessary to carry on business or employment.
- Pensions – almost every kind is now sacrosanct.
- Ongoing income up to the level you need to keep up a reasonable standard of living for yourself and family. This is very much a moveable feast as the word 'reasonable' is loosely applied according to individual circumstances.

? **What if I go bankrupt and then win a car or a moderate cash amount? (Let's assume that if you win the double rollover you won't mind reimbursing your creditors.)**

From the date of your bankruptcy order to the date you're discharged (usually one year, but it can vary) you must notify and hand over what's called 'after-acquired property' – effectively anything you didn't own before the bankruptcy and excluding income afterwards. There's no minimum value but cash or goods worth under £500 are usually ignored.

The most common sources of 'after-acquired' property are legacies, gifts and winnings from games of skill or chance.

Obviously if whatever you might inherit, be given, or win is worth vastly more than the total of your bankruptcy debts and costs you can keep the change, but don't be surprised if those debts and costs turn out to be a lot higher than you expected.

? **I've got medical insurance and want to know this: My policy will pay out £100K if I'm unlucky enough to contract bacterial meningitis. But say this happens during my bankruptcy; who gets the money then?**

If you fall ill or have a serious accident, the bankruptcy gets whatever part of any compensation you might be awarded, which relates to financial matters such as loss of earnings. The only bits you get to keep are those that might cover your own distress – often not very much unfortunately.

? **If I go bankrupt will my spouse's assets and income be taken into account?**

No – he or she can't be held responsible in any way, though sometimes a trustee in bankruptcy may look closely into how he or she came by those assets.

? **I've got four kids, a dog and a three-legged cat to support – surely our home can't be taken from us if I go bankrupt?**

Your house is certainly one of the assets which vest automatically in the bankruptcy and your trustee will be very keen to extract the most he can from it. If your house is pretty much mortgaged up to the hilt the trustee won't be quite so bothered, but that doesn't mean you should assume he will stay that way. He will keep an eye on its value and will pounce if it begins to look worthwhile. But it's worth noting that if he's done nothing for three years it reverts to you anyway.

If the trustee has reason to believe the house is worth a lot more than the mortgages over it, he or she will write to you (and your co-owner if it is jointly owned) setting out various options for you to retrieve the house, such as for your co-owner to buy the bankruptcy's interest by getting a bigger mortgage. If you can't or won't agree to one or other of the options offered to you the trustee will go to court to get an order evicting you and your family so that the house can be sold.

? **I know I'm the sole beneficiary in Great Aunt Flo's will and what's more her sell-by date is fast approaching. What if I inherit all her worldly goods whilst I'm bankrupt?**

It is after-acquired property – you lose it all, at least up to the total bankruptcy debts and costs.

? **I've been made bankrupt, will I ever get a mortgage, a loan or a credit card again?**

Of course you will: your credit rating repairs itself in six years or so, and though you can often get such things in less time, you'll be paying through the nose because of being seen as a pretty poor risk.

It is ultra important, however, to remember that until you're discharged you must not try to borrow money without telling your intended lender you're in bankruptcy – if you don't, you can easily find yourself in the slammer.

? **I've lost my home through bankruptcy and now I need to rent. How can I do this when I'll automatically fail the estate agents' credit check?**

This is not easy short of shelling out a large deposit and advance rent. Sometimes the way the home is lost can be used to help you jump local authority public housing queues.

? ** **I've been declared bankrupt. Will my current bank account be taken from me?

If you use that account just for your income and outgoings and if you don't have any overdraft on it you'll usually be allowed to keep it, provided, of course, the bank doesn't mind you staying a customer. Often it's a good idea to open a fallback account in case your bankruptcy makes your existing bank not love you any more.

12

Wendy's Way To Save A Wad

Planning Ahead is Just the Ticket

First off, never, *ever* (apart from medical emergencies) make the London to Manchester train journey without having bought a ticket beforehand. Of course this caution against buying your ticket on board will apply to many other inter-city journeys but it's the London to Stoke-on-Trent leg I am the most familiar with. Some years ago I would have advised exactly the opposite; more often than not a seat in first class could be taken and a pleasant journey could be had without fear of any interruption from an on-board conductor – they simply didn't come around to check your ticket. Nowadays, it's quite a different story. Gary and I plonked ourselves down in first class one day and when the conductor asked for our non-existent tickets I simply asked him if I could purchase two Stoke to London returns. Of course we could – at a total cost of £450! Wincing but not wanting to move, I duly handed over my gold Amex card… and we wonder where all our money has gone! That very painful occasion must have been the first and last time I paid out the full fare, although it was not the last time I travelled on the train first class. The simple purchase of an Apex fare a week or two in advance of your journey will ensure that you can enjoy the pleasures of a first class seat at a fraction of the open fare cost. Not only that but you can pig out on the free food trolley and get pissed on the free booze. For added comfort and value for money always travel with an unruly toddler: your fellow travellers will soon drift off into another carriage and you'll have a whole first class coach to yourself!

Bargain Booty – Cutting Back Without Dumbing Down

Now I love a bargain as much as the next person. No, that's wrong. I enjoy a bargain more than anyone else I know. I always have done. Even in the days when my wallet would practically be aglow with gold, I would get immense pleasure from rooting out a bargain from a market stall, a charity shop or a car boot sale. Years ago one might have done that kind of thing in a rather covert manner, but once again times have changed. A second hand item can be referred to as an 'antique', and a garment purchased from a charity shop may be described with some confidence as 'vintage'. So, next time you're in town try strutting into Help the Aged with all the conviction and authority of someone who is well used to unearthing classic Chanel for £2.50. And don't forget the book section: there's always the chance that a first edition du Maurier will be nestling alongside the Mills & Boon.

This holding-your-head-up-high-in-a-cheap-shop principle has really come into its own in recent times. Not so long ago I walked into a Primark – the Kingston-upon-Thames branch, which boasts three glorious floors of fashionable must haves. Combats for a fiver, stylish PJs for £4, boots to die for for £10, kids' T-shirts for £1 – why on earth had I stayed a Primark virgin for so long? Spend £50 here and you'll depart the shop laden down with more bags of goodies than you can carry! When you're on a tight budget, the likes of Primark, Tesco and T.K. Maxx are a clothing oasis in the fashion retail desert.

Look After the Pennies – the Pounds Really Will Look After Themselves

Coin Star! It feels like winning the jackpot! I discovered the Coin Star machine in our local Sainsbury's after having a rather embarrassing episode with a carrier bag full of change. After having amassed a ridiculous amount of coppers and silver coins I decided to take it all down to the bank, working on the assumption that they would have some kind of machine that sorted it all out and counted it all up for you. My carrier bag of change was so heavy that I reinforced it with two other carriers and enlisted Gary's help to heave it into the bank. It soon transpired that I was meant to sort out the coinage myself, a task that quite frankly I couldn't be arsed to do. Tutting and cursing, we carried our bag of money back to the car. By that time, however, the coins and the carriers had had enough. The bag couldn't take the strain any longer and the coins wanted out. If only they could have waited until they were safely in the boot before making their bid for freedom. Scrabbling around on your hands and knees, chasing small change in Twickenham town centre, is not for the proud or faint-hearted! So traumatised was I by the whole escapade that the rotten old coins in their torn and useless old bag stayed in the boot of the car for some twelve months. Until I discovered Coin Star. This miracle of a machine swallows up all your change and totals it up before spitting out a voucher for the full amount (less 7% handling fee) at the end. You can use the voucher at the store or simply turn it into notes! It's so easy but ultimately the point I am making is this: I had always assumed that the bag of coins in question would total something like £70 and Gary's estimate was along the same lines. Imagine our surprise and delight therefore when a trip to Coin Star revealed that the small change totalled some £280! Raid your old coat pockets and turf all the cushions off the sofa; in every pot of change there are notes just bursting to get out!

How to Play the Market and Always Come Out on Top!

Do you have a local market? Because if the answer is 'yes' it is undoubtedly hiding a treasure trove of bargains! If I'm ever at my mum and dad's on a Wednesday I'm up and out of bed and champing at the bit to get to Leek Market. OK, your market may not have the same things that Leek Market has but the principle of discovery is the same. The Sock Man – the one who sells M&S socks at a quarter of the cost. The Jumper Lady – the one who sells end of range jumpers from George to Whistles, all at £3 each. Then there's The Shoe Man – the one who sells pink mock Timberlands for a tenner. And The Fruit & Veg Man – the one who sells five avocados for a pound. *Five avocados for a pound?!* I'm in guacamole heaven! Even the 'every little helps' brigade can't compete with the likes of that! Still, talking of supermarkets, how about this one: rapeseed oil! Allegedly it's better for you than olive oil and better still it's just 99p for a whole litre! Probably less if you care to shop around...

Surf Your Way to Cheaper Living – Get Online and Get on Target

Lastly, never, *ever* pay the rack rate for a hotel room (i.e. the rate that is posted up behind the hotel reception). Thank God for the internet. Never before has it been so easy to secure a super duper room at a super duper price. But beware! On several occasions I have booked a room at a down and dirty rate only to discover that the room is, well, down and dirty. The big chain hotels are the worst offenders for this, giving you their grotty 'standby' rooms because you've paid a low price on the net for it. This quickly becomes shoddy practice when the info on the web leads you to believe you're booking one of the hotel's standard rooms, with no mention in the blurb that upon arrival you'll be given the key to a room, which hasn't been refurbished since The Bay City Rollers were booming. This is the time to push one's British reserve firmly to one side, go down to reception and *demand* loudly that you be transferred to a room worthy of the hotel's famous name. Never was the contrast more vivid than when this happened to us at The Hilton Hotel in Brighton. We went from under the arches to Buck Palace in the simple swipe of a key card! Never be diddled on quality... it's your hard earned cash you're parting with after all.

Wendy Turner

Epilogue

Whilst writing this epilogue about an extremely stressful but enlightening year, I am reminded of that great sound bite that accompanied the publicity circus of the opening of the film *Jaws 2* in 1978 – *Just when you thought it was safe to get back in the water...* Meaning: just when you thought it was all over it just might not be! I say this because I thought I had finished my year of woe at Chapter 10 until my publishers got on the phone and informed me that something was missing ... a gap needed filling... *we need to know what happened next!*

And after some thinking, they are right. It's alright me telling everyone to remain positive through what can be extremely negative times, or extol the virtues of humour in very unfortunate circumstances. But where is the pay off? The punch line? What happens if you do all those things? Does it make life any easier? Well, yes, I can assure you it does. Once declared bankrupt things do take on a more measured and manageable feel. This is primarily due to the fact that many things are taken out of your hands and put into those of a trustee who works on behalf of your creditors (those you owe money to), but also for you as well. They are there to make sure that you are not pulling a fast one, but also to make sure no one is giving you any undeserved pressure.

They will assess your earnings if you are working but will not leave you poverty stricken or unable to meet your day-to-day expenditure. Your incomings must cover your outgoings and only then can any creditors potentially see the colour of your money. If you happen to have a sizeable Lottery win whilst being bankrupt prepare for those winnings to be taken into consideration. The one thing that can be contentious is your property if you own some. Your family home will eventually be included in the sale of assets but if you have children of school age you may stay in your home for up to twelve months as long as you can cover the mortgage repayments. This at least gives you some breathing space and time to make new plans.

In going bankrupt, a lot of stress and worry went too. No more debt collectors applying pressure, no more constant phone calls, no more long sessions of working out how to keep everyone happy and live a family life at the same time. I knew it was the end of one era and the start of another. During this year of bankruptcy Wendy and I decided to take this opportunity to make sure we never have to live through the tough times again. We decided to start to fulfil our potential or at least to give it the best shot we could; to be proactive in a way we had never been before. At least we would know that if we ever got into financial trouble again it wouldn't be because we didn't care about our situation or had suffered from the ostrich syndrome – you got it – burying our heads in the sand. No, we would use this whole experience to start afresh, to kick-start our lives in a way that meant we were more in control and not always waiting around for someone else to employ us or determine our fate. It would now be in our own hands.

I think this can apply to anyone who has been in a similar situation. I would encourage any dreams to be pursued – even if it's just attending council run art classes once a week because for years you've wanted to recapture the thrill you felt at school but were always too weighed down by financial worry to give it a go. Or how about submitting a long held idea to TV's *Dragon's Den*! If you think you can't, you won't, so just get out there and do it! We've all had a rude awakening but life is there for the taking.

So, one year on, and out of bankruptcy, watching my wife put the finishing touches to her first novel, sitting at our old table in our really cool *rented* house, I am also putting the finishing touches to this, my first book. Wendy and I are also in negotiations to do an informative TV series about bankruptcy and to offer our help and advice to others who are going through it. The TV series and this book are here to say there is light at the end of the tunnel. It can be done, and if I can do it, anyone can! There is nothing to fear… there are new challenges to be faced and what is past is past. Of course, lessons have to be learned but once they have then anything is possible. Some of the most successful people in the world today have been bankrupt, so we are not alone.

In closing (and I really mean it this time), whatever form your new start takes, remember what the great Winston Churchill said: 'Every no takes you closer to a yes.' And for myself, I once again go back to where I came in with: *Your altitude is determined by your attitude.* If you can keep positive, keep together and keep perspective you will not only survive bankruptcy but make it the catalyst for a new start for the rest of your life.

Appendix – Useful Contacts

Citizens' Advice Bureau
There are 3,000 centres nationwide. Find your nearest CAB at www.citizensadvice.org.uk or in your local phone directory. Online advice is also available at www.adviceguide.org.uk.

Consumer Credit Counselling Service
A national charity offering debt advice.
www.cccs.co.uk
0800 138 1111

National Debtline
Another national advice charity, this one run by the Money Advice Trust.
www.nationaldebtline.co.uk
0808 808 4000

The Samaritans
Advice and support on a huge range of subjects.
www.samaritans.org.uk
08457 90 90 90

The Association of Business Recovery Professionals
Most Insolvency Practitioners belong to this association, which publishes numerous guides and is able to direct

enquirers to their nearest/most suitable Insolvency Practitioner for specific advice.
www.r3.org.uk

Tenon Debt Solutions
Ian Cadlock, who provided the expert financial advice for this book, is an Insolvency Practitioner at the Tenon Group.
www.tenondebtsolutions.com
0808 238 0101